COMMUNING WITH CHRIST

A Thirty-One Day
Communion Devotional

Cheryl Weathermon McNeil

PRAISE FOR
"COMMUNING WITH CHRIST"

While reading the devotions in **Communing with Christ**, we have become absolutely sure that the Lord directed Cheryl McNeil in the writing of this book. There is such a need for this material, not only for pastors and those in leadership, but for all Christians to help them realize the significance of this sacred remembrance. We are thankful that Cheryl obeyed the prompting of the Holy Spirit, and we applaud her for following his voice.

Buford and Lana Ness
Senior Pastors, Church on the Beach, Salinas, Ecuador

I have been in church my entire life, taking communion in many denominations and geographic locations. Often, I must admit, it has been a ritual I experienced without always reflecting on its meaning. Cheryl McNeil, in her exhaustive study of this important celebration, has given me much food for thought regarding the substance of the Eucharist. I highly recommend her **Communing with Christ** as a spiritual guide to a deeper understanding of the Lord's Supper.

Susie Wilson DMA

Communing with Christ is a book of 31 devotionals written to help the reader fully participate in different aspects of the Lord's Supper. Cheryl McNeil clearly brings to life the words and actions of Jesus during his last Passover season. Whether taking Communion alone or receiving Communion in a group, this book will invite you to a deeper understanding and purpose of this blessed and holy celebration.

Don Hopkins
Pastor, Christian Family Church Dallas

Communing with Christ is a powerful dive into a daily experience of taking the bread and the cup. Many aspects of taking communion are not expounded upon from the pulpit. These secret truths have been carefully laid out for the reader. Each day is a new revelation and a new experience. The Word of God comes alive as we begin to understand the promises we have through the broken body of Jesus and the power of his blood. Cheryl McNeil has delicately placed these promises of God into every day of this beautifully written book. Take this 31-day journey and experience revelation and intimacy with the Father like never before.

Kristyn Jones, D.C.
Healing Pointe Chiropractic, Sachse, Texas

Communing with Christ is a life changing book that instills peace and knowledge into its readers. Personally, as I read the book, I saw it as more of a tool to help those who are not familiar with Christ to learn more about Him. It also helps educate experienced Christians in their walk with the Lord as well. This wonderful devotional serves as a guide to help the reader discover a stronger and deeper relationship with Jesus Christ as Lord and Savior. We as Christians strive daily to be more like Jesus and to be a mirror image of who He was, and this devotional helps to attain that goal. *Communing with Christ* is a powerful testament of how we should remember and embrace God's presence in our lives every day. "He, who hath an ear to hear, let him hear."

John Graham
India Tribals In Ministry, Mesquite, Texas

Scripture Quotations of the Holy Bible Used in this Publication Are as Follows:

Italics, colored print, and highlights added to Scripture quotations reflect the author's own emphasis.

CONTENTS

WHAT IS COMMUNION?

Communion is an ordinance celebrated by the Christian Church. It was instituted by Christ himself in an upper room in Jerusalem when he and his followers met together to share in a Passover Meal just before Jesus was to die on the cross to atone for the sins of man.

The ordinance is also known as the Lord's Supper and uses two elements in the meal - bread to remind us of the broken body of Christ and wine to remind us of the blood that was poured out from Christ's tortured body.

Communion calls us to remembrance.
Communion celebrates the 'new covenant'.
Communion points to a future, eternal life with Christ.

Communion, the Lord's Supper, should never be neglected. Jesus commanded that we should continue to partake of the elements in remembrance of him.

The Communion celebration is a meaningful, important activity that should always be a part of the Christian's worship.

Jesus said,
*"Do this in remembrance of me." **(Luke 22:19)***

Let us be obedient to our Savior's instructions.

INTRODUCTION

I grew up attending a protestant, evangelical church and our monthly *Communion* service was a special time set aside for each first Sunday. When the pastor would lead us into this beautiful time of remembrance, there was no hurry to get through the ceremony. Scriptures were read, words about Jesus' gift of salvation were spoken, and often a song was sung before we ever got to the partaking of the elements themselves. Tears were shed in remembrance of what Jesus did for us and in repentance for wrongs we may have committed in the living of our daily lives. It was a solemn time and we felt the presence of our Savior as we assembled together to remember him.

Through the years in the different churches we have attended, I have noticed a concerning change in the time taken for the ordinance and in the solemnity with which it is approached. It has become a time that feels rushed, irreverent, and misunderstood. Often, it is a quickly inserted part of the service with no time for Scriptures to be read and no time to consider Christ and his ultimate sacrifice. As I have questioned the current methods by which *Communion* is served or received, one of my desires has been to make sure that I myself am keeping the ordinance in a manner that pleases Christ.

It was out of my search to improve my own participation in the *Lord's Supper* that this book was born. I sincerely wanted to have a greater understanding of what I should be considering and what I should be doing as I gathered with other believers to partake of the *Communion* elements. I wanted to delve into some of the processes, activities, actions, responses, and understandings that take place in the celebration of *Communion*. Although there are others to be considered, the thirty-one days of devotionals that I have chosen seem to be good descriptions of what it means to come to *The Table* and partake.

My goal in writing this devotional is to help us take the time to really remember and express our gratitude and love for the One who gave his all, for the One who sacrificed himself so that we might live.

Jesus said, *"Do this, as often as you drink it, in remembrance of me."* Now scripture does not say, "Do this often," but I believe that is the implied meaning. These thirty-one days will be a great start in helping us to realize how important the 'often' is. There are so many benefits that we can receive as we partake of the *Lord's Supper.* These devotionals are intended to awaken us to these many blessings and to give us a better understanding of why Jesus commanded us to remember him through the *Sacrament of Communion.* The studies may be used as daily devotionals but can also be used once a month or as a weekly Bible study. And, although Communion is meant to be taken as a 'together' time, it is perfectly all right to use these devotionals in your own private prayer moments. I pray that as you go from one lesson to the next, your connection with *Communion* and with our Savior will grow and expand as we await our Bridegroom's soon return.

(For the purpose of this book, the following terms may be used interchangeably and considered synonymous to Communion: Last Supper, Lord's Supper, Eucharist, Holy Meal, First Supper, Communion Table, Holy Communion, Sacrament, Holy Sacrament, and Covenant Meal.)

DAY ONE: *COMMUNING WITH CHRIST THROUGH REMEMBERING*

When Jesus reclined around the *Passover Table* with his disciples and instituted the *Ordinance of Communion*, he exhorted them to partake of the emblems, of the bread and of the cup, in *remembrance* of him. In *remembrance*!

Jesus used the words *remember* and *remembrance* less than a dozen times while teaching his disciples. He used the words to **recall and warn**, as when he admonished, *"Remember Lot's wife.";* to **reprimand,** as when he said to his followers, *"Don't you remember?"* (a question pertaining to the miracles he had performed but which the disciples seemed to have quickly forgotten); and to **remind**, as found in *I Corinthians 11:23-25 (NLT),* which are the verses of Scripture which record the Lord's words when he shared the elements with those gathered for the *Passover Meal*. This **reminding** encourages us to *remember*.

Paul writes, *"On the night when he was betrayed, the Lord Jesus took some bread and gave thanks to God for it. Then he broke it in pieces and said, 'This is my body, which is given for you. Do this in remembrance of me.' In the same way, he took the cup of wine after supper, saying, 'This cup is the new covenant between God and his people—an agreement confirmed with my blood. Do this in remembrance of me as often as you drink it.'"* And with these words, Jesus was **reminding** us to *remember* him.

What brings about *remembrance*? A sight, a sound, a taste or smell, a texture of something felt? Or perhaps a sudden thought? Yes, all of these. And often memories do **just happen** when one of our senses is awakened. But a sudden *remembrance* is not what Jesus had in mind. He wanted us to **intentionally** *remember* Him, to *remember* **on purpose** the sacrifice that he has provided for us. Jesus wanted us to understand and embrace his death with the full knowledge that it was his death that purchased our salvation; it was his death that brings us back into fellowship with a Holy God.

Today, when we want to *remember* on purpose, we might pull out some pictures or look them up on an electronic device. We might read a note or letter, talk with someone else who was 'there', open a special bottle of perfume, listen to a sentimental song, or look at or touch an object which brings back special, important memories. Jesus understood that we as human beings would need something concrete to use as a **reminder** of the gift he provided for us at Calvary when he laid down his life by the breaking of his body and the spilling of his blood. And so, **he reminded us to** *remember* **him**, and that is done through taking the *Communion elements*. Just as Jesus partook of the bread and the fruit of the vine on the night he was betrayed, we also have these elements to take into our bodies as a **reminder** of his great love for us and to help us to *remember* that he is our everything; we live and breathe because of him for he provides all the nourishment (symbolized by the bread and the cup) that we need to sustain life.

A Prayer for Remembering

Dear Lord, as we partake of the elements signifying your body that was broken and your blood that was spilled, help us to *remember* that you did it all because of your great love for us. Help us to *remember* that without the precious gift you provided for us at Calvary, we would not be able to be in right relationship with our Father. And help us to *remember* the pain and suffering you experienced so that we might have eternal life. We thank you and honor you at this Holy time and pray these things in your name, Jesus, the name above all names. Amen.

And now, as we intentionally remember the great sacrifice our Lord and Savior made for us, let us eat of the bread and drink of the cup of the vine as we experience Holy Communion.

Doxology

Oh, let me always *remember*, Lord,
the sacrifice you gave.
And may the *memory* of your great gift
open my heart to your amazing love
and be forever full of praise.

4

Communing
WITH
CHRIST

DAY TWO: *COMMUNING WITH CHRIST THROUGH COMMEMORATING*

Today we study *Communion* as a time of *commemorating*. A *commemoration* is a ceremony set aside to remember a **person** or an **event,** or **both.** By partaking of the elements of the bread and the cup, we *commemorate*, we celebrate, **the person (Jesus Christ),** and the **event, (his death on the cross)** through whom and by which our salvation was purchased.

Jesus told us to do this. And at the table, he spoke about a new covenant which would soon be available to replace the old covenant. The old covenant (or Mosaic Covenant) was one which God made with Israel after freeing his people from the bondage of Egypt and giving them his special laws to uphold. This covenant was established and ratified, and Israel's freedom was *commemorated* by the shedding of the blood of animals. But this covenant, this special agreement between God and man, was an incomplete one. As stated in **Exodus 19:8 (KJV),** the people had agreed to keep the law, and had even declared with their words, *"All that the Lord has spoken we will do!"* And although God, who is always trustworthy and unfailing, kept his word, the people were not able to keep their part of the agreement. If the Israelites could not follow the covenant rules, what were they to do?

Jesus became the answer. At the final *Passover Meal* he would share with his disciples, he told them that his death would bring about a **new covenant**, a covenant in **HIS** blood, not the blood of lambs or goats but of **THE ONE, THE CHRIST**, who was unblemished, spotless, and whose blood truly could cleanse and purify them. And so, when Jesus shared this special meal with his disciples on the night of his arrest, he broke the bread and lifted the cup and said,

*"This bread is my body that I am giving for you. Eat this to remember me…. This wine represents the new agreement from God to his people. It will begin when my blood is poured out for you." **Luke 22:19-20 (ERV)***

Through our acknowledgement of Christ's death and resurrection and our acceptance of the gift he so willingly provided, we now have victory over sin! His blood cleanses us; it justifies us; it redeems us! There is **power in the blood of Jesus Christ, the perfect sacrificial lamb!** What we as mere mortals could not do, Jesus willingly did for us!

In Hebrews, we read that the death of Jesus on the cross brought about a **'better covenant'**. This covenant is perfect. It is complete. It is forever. Jesus did the hard work; his part in the covenant cost him everything: his life, his glory, and separation from Heaven and his Father. Our part in the covenant requires only that we repent and believe. How wonderful that God loved us so much that he would enter into this incomparable covenant with us!

Let us now celebrate this new and **better covenant** as we *commemorate* the ***Holy Person Jesus, the Son of God,*** and the ***special event***, **the sacrifice of his life** for us, his beloved creation.

A Prayer for Commemorating

Dear Lord Jesus, as we come into your presence, we *commemorate* you and we *commemorate* what you did for us on the cross. We praise you for the opportunity to join together as a body of believers to remember and to thank you. In your name we pray. Amen.

As we partake of the bread and the vine in this solemn and blessed moment, let us commemorate our Lord and his death and worship our Savior for all he did for us at Calvary. We remember the <u>Savior</u> and we remember the <u>Sacrifice</u>.

Doxology

When I eat of the bread and drink of the vine,
I find great contentment in *commemorating* you.
The new covenant you signed
with your own precious blood
gives me hope for the future.
Let me never forget!

DAY THREE: *COMMUNING WITH CHRIST THROUGH AGREEING*

When we read the words of Jesus in **Mark 14:24 (ERV)**, we see that he was explaining the connection between the wine he was about to pour out and share with his disciples and his own blood which he would soon pour out to be spilled for all mankind. Scripture provides Jesus' words: *"This wine is my blood, which will be poured out for many to begin the new agreement from God to his people."* In the *(ICB)*, the translation reads, *"Then Jesus said, 'This is my blood which begins the new agreement that God makes with his people. This blood is poured out for many.'* And in the *(WE)*, Scripture states, *"Then he said to them, `This is my blood. It is given for many people. It makes the agreement strong.'"* Christ's blood sealed the *agreement*.

While at the *Passover Table*, Jesus spoke of an *agreement* that was to be made by God with his people, and he called it a *new agreement*. This is in contrast to the **old** *agreement*, the *covenant* that was understood and used by the priests in the Old Testament. The **old** *covenant* was incomplete, imperfect, and temporary. This *new agreement* about which Christ spoke was an indestructible *agreement*, one that did not have to be repeated year after year but was a one-time event. It was the complete fulfillment of God's ultimate plan for his creation. The priest no longer had to go into the Holy of Holies each year; no commanded, detailed preparation had to take place; and no special garments were required in order for man to enter God's presence. For when Jesus' blood was shed, the **old** *covenant* became obsolete and its actions were no longer needed to bring about man's redemption.

Covenant is the word used in the **Mark 14** text of many translations of the Bible. It is used in New Testament Scriptures when comparing the *agreement* under which the Israelites labored to be free from sin to the *covenant* about which our Savior spoke when he instituted the observance of *Communion*. *"He said to them, 'This is my blood, which seals the new covenant poured out for many.'" (TPT)*

In the **Good News Translation,** we read, *"Jesus said, 'This is my blood which is poured out for many, my blood which seals God's covenant.'"*

And the term *new testament* is used in the **King James Version** to speak of the *new agreement*. *"And he said unto them, 'This is my blood of the new testament, which is shed for many.'"*

Jesus speaks of his blood as the inscription with which this *new agreement*, this *new testament*, this *new covenant* was signed. In agreeing to remove our sins through the *new covenant*, he signed it in his own precious blood which made it a complete, unbreakable, immutable *agreement*. In **Jeremiah 31:33 (NIV)**, the Lord declares: *"This is the covenant I will make with (my) people,' declares the* LORD. *'I will put my law in their minds and write it on their hearts. I will be their God, and they will be my people.'"*.

The *agreement* has been made. It has been signed in the blood of our Lord, and if we also *agree* and come to him in faith believing, this permanent *covenant* will be written on our hearts.

A Prayer for Agreeing

Oh, Father God, we come to you in *agreement* with the *covenant* you made on our behalf. We accept the love you showed so fully by sending your Son to be broken and to bleed and to die that we might be in *covenant* relationship with you. We want to be your children, and we accept you as our God through Jesus Christ, our Lord. Amen.

Today, as we partake of the bread and the cup, let us come in agreement and enjoin ourselves to God in the covenant made through the blood of his son Jesus, our Lord and Savior. Amen.

Doxology

In receiving your new *covenant*,
I find my heart has strokes of red
written in the blood of Christ.
This permanent ink
can never be removed.
Your *agreement* makes it so.

DAY FOUR: *COMMUNING WITH CHRIST THROUGH EXCHANGING*

In the midst of all the pain and suffering Jesus experienced when he died on the cross, there were miraculous *exchanges* that were taking place and provided through Christ on our behalf. In the making of the new covenant brought about by the death of his own dear Son, God effected divine *exchanges* with us, his prized creation. Christ loved us so much that he willingly took the **bad** that we had inherited through Adam's fall and **did deserve and** *exchanged* it with the **good** that he had planned for us which we **did not deserve.** Though definitely not a full list, four of these *exchanges* stand out when considering the loving plan God had for those he created in his own image.

1) Because of our sins, we deserve **punishment,** but through Christ's death, we receive **forgiveness.** In **Ephesians 1:7 (KJV),** we read, *"In whom we have redemption through his blood, the **forgiveness** of sins, according to the riches of his grace."* And in **Isaiah 53:5 (NCV),** this *exchange* is made clear: *"But he was wounded for the wrong we did; he was crushed for the evil we did. The **punishment,** which made us well, was given to him."* **Forgiveness** instead of **punishment** - an incomprehensible *trade-off.*

2) Because of our sins, we deserve God's total, irrevocable **rejection,** but through the cross, we receive complete, inconceivable **acceptance.** It is amazing that God **accepts** us,

that he even cared enough to bring us back into fellowship with him. But he did care, and at what a cost! It was necessary that he **abandon** his own Son and because of that, Christ took the **rejection** that should have been ours. He was **rejected** by those around him and **forsaken** by his Father, all in order that we might be **accepted** into the Kingdom of God. When he was dying on the cross, he called out to his Father and shouted, *"My God, my God, why have you **deserted** me?" **Matthew 27:46 (CEV).** **Ephesians 1:5 (GW)** explains: *"Because of his love he had already decided to adopt us through Jesus Christ. He freely chose to do this."* And so, we are no longer **rejected**; we are no longer slaves. We have been **accepted** as sons and daughters of the Most High God! What a glorious *exchange*!

3) Because of our sins, we deserve **curses,** but because Jesus took the **curse** for us, we receive God's **blessings.** **Galatians 3:13-14 (KJV)** speaks of this wonderful *exchange*: *"Christ hath redeemed us from the **curse** of the law, being made a **curse** for us: that the **blessing** of Abraham might come on the Gentiles through Jesus Christ."* When we come to Christ and accept him as Lord and Savior, the **curses** that should have been ours are replaced by the glorious **blessings** of peace, joy, and salvation. **Blessings** for **curses** - an awesome *transaction*!

4) Because of our sins, we deserve **death,** but because of Christ's great gift on the cross, we can receive **eternal life**. In **John 3:16 (KJV)** we read, *"For God so loved the world, that he gave his only begotten Son, that whosoever believeth in him should not perish (die) but have everlasting life."* The sting of **death** is *exchanged* for **eternal life** with Christ.

When we come to the *Communion Table* to consider Christ's sacrifice of love, we should also remember the **punishment,** *rejection, curses,* and ***death*** that should have been ours. But because Christ instead took them on himself, we can be eternally grateful for the wonderful *replacement* gifts of ***forgiveness, acceptance, blessings,*** and ***eternal life*** that we can receive through Jesus Christ our Lord.

We now read the *Communion* Scriptures. *"While they were eating, Jesus took bread, and when he had given thanks, he broke it and gave it to his disciples, saying, 'Take and eat; this is my body.' Then he took a cup, and when he had given thanks, he gave it to them, saying, 'Drink from it, all of you. This is my blood of the covenant, which is poured out for many for the forgiveness of sins.'" **Matthew 26:26-28 (CSB)***

A Prayer for Exchanging

Father, as we come to *Your Table*, we are grateful that we have been *forgiven*. Thank you for offering us *acceptance, blessings*, and *eternal life* through the amazing *exchanges* provided by the death of your Son. Amen.

Let us now partake of the Lord's Supper and be reminded of the great exchanges that took place because of the cross.

Doxology

You took the death reserved for me;
You gave me life that I might see
that your *exchanges*
have made me free.
Forgiven!

DAY FIVE: *COMMUNING WITH CHRIST THROUGH PROCLAIMING*

Today as we prepare to partake of the *Lord's Supper*, I want us to be drawn to the words of Jesus as he was reminding his disciples of the importance of sharing in the ordinance of *Communion*. He admonished them to take the bread and the wine to remember him and his soon-coming death at Calvary.

Then Jesus told them to receive the emblems in order to *"...proclaim the Lord's death until he comes."* **I Corinthians 11:26 (ESV).** Yes, we are to remember, but we are also to *proclaim*. *Communion* is a time of **testimony**! It is a time of reminding ourselves and *proclaiming* to others the real reason Jesus came to the earth: He came to die. That sounds ominous and indeed it is. Although Christ is God, the **Giver of Life**, he came to **offer up his own life**, to be put to death just like any common criminal. He didn't have to die; he chose to. And some who watched him die didn't believe that a true God would allow himself to be killed in such a horrendous manner. Many mocked him because of his claim to be God.

Think about this: When Jesus prayed in the garden, his heart nearly breaking, he didn't **feel** like a god. When he was tortured, his body broken and his blood spilled, he didn't **look** like a god. When he was nailed to the cross and cried out to his Father, he didn't **sound** like a god. And when he died and was laid in another man's tomb, he wasn't **buried** like a God. Yes, Jesus the man, **was dead**, but this dead man **was still**

18

God which was proven by his powerful resurrection. In death, he had accomplished his greatest mission – the redemption of mankind! In *I Peter 2:9 (VOICE),* we are reminded of our **position** and our **purpose** through our relationship with Christ. Peter writes, *"But you are a **chosen people**; ...so that you may proclaim the wondrous acts of the One who called you out of inky darkness into shimmering light."* Because of what Christ accomplished on the cross, we are **chosen** by him to *proclaim* his death.

To Jesus, it was important that we would remember his death but it was also important that we would *show forth* his death, that we would *proclaim* his death. He wanted us to use the time of *Communion* as a time of *proclamation.* When I think of **proclaiming**, I think of stating something very forcefully so that others will hear and understand it. When we *proclaim* the Lord's death, we are emphatically and unequivocally telling others that Jesus' death had a purpose. And in the repetition of *Communion*, the regular taking of the *Lord's Supper,* we are **testifying** of God's great love for us.

Now as we come to the *Lord's Table*, we read the words of Christ that Paul shared with us in *I Corinthians 11:23-26 (GW):*

*"On the night he was betrayed, the Lord Jesus took bread and spoke a prayer of thanksgiving. He broke the bread and said, 'This is my body, which is given for you. Do this to remember me.' When supper was over, he did the same with the cup. He said, 'This cup is the new promise made with my blood. Every time you drink from it, do it to remember me. Every time you eat this bread and drink from this cup, you **tell about** the Lord's death until he comes.'"*

Jesus knew the importance of *proclaiming* his death – the importance for him, the importance for us. As we take of the elements, we should also consider how blessed we are that we can *testify* of the great love Jesus showed through his death at Calvary.

A Prayer for Proclaiming

Dear Lord Jesus, we thank you for your death that brings salvation to our weary souls. We want to *stand up* for you, to *testify* of you, to *proclaim* the great gift you gave through your death on the cross. Today, as we take of the elements of the bread and the cup, let our hearts jump in jubilation that we have this opportunity to *proclaim* what your death offers to all who believe. In your name we pray. Amen.

As we come now to partake of the elements, to experience the Lord's Supper, let it be a time of proclamation. We proclaim his death and what his death has done for those who have accepted him as Savior and are following him as Lord.

Doxology

Today, I *testify* of your great love.
As I take of these emblems,
I *proclaim* your death.
For out of your death,
I have been given life.
Life everlasting!

DAY SIX: *COMMUNING WITH CHRIST*
THROUGH ENTERING

Being able to *enter* into God's presence is so much a part of the *Communion Service* that we sometimes forget that we can only do that because of Jesus. It happens because of the ultimate act of love Jesus provided for us when he died on the cross.

Before Jesus' death, the common man had no direct access to God. Only the high priest could *enter* into the Holy of Holies, the special veiled place where God's glory dwelled, and the priest could *enter* this place only on one pre-determined day of the year - the Day of Atonement. This ritual required elaborate actions and specific preparations to be made by the high priest before even he could *enter* this place of God's presence. He could only go into this sacred place by going behind a veil of separation. There were many steps the priest had to take, and he had to be very careful to follow them exactly or risk death. That was how important this ceremony was. But why was this all necessary? We see in Scripture that a Holy God could not bear to look on the sins of an unjust, unholy people. He wanted fellowship with his creation, he wanted to absolve them of their sin, and this was the way he had chosen for the atonement to take place.

Remember, in this Old Testament ceremony, only the high priest could *enter* the Holy Place. But everything changed when Jesus came, and walked among men, and taught in the temple, and **died**. He became the final sacrificial Lamb for the redemption of mankind. No longer was the annual ritual of sacrificing an unblemished lamb required; no longer was the veil an instrument of separation that hung between God and man; no longer did man have to depend on another imperfect, created being to absolve him of sin. No! Our Lord and Savior paved the way for us to be able *to go directly into* God's presence. And at the time of *Communion*, we who have believed on the Son of God can *enter* into the Holy of Holies and receive mercy as we partake of the emblems of the bread and the wine. We can do this because the veil no longer constrains us; it no longer separates us; it no longer forbids us to come into the presence of Jehovah God. Because the veil was torn when Jesus died on the cross, we can come boldly before the Father and be surrounded by the love that can only come from the Triune God.

And so, as we reach for the broken bread and embrace the cup of the vine, we step into God's Holy Presence and receive love, mercy, forgiveness, and redemption. We remember that when Christ's body was torn, the veil to the temple was also torn giving us access to a person-to-person relationship with him.

Matthew 27:51 (TLB) reads, *"And look! The curtain secluding the Holiest Place in the Temple was split apart from top to bottom,"* allowing all who would come to *enter* into the presence of the Holy One.

The *Communion* Scriptures help to draw us into this Holy time of remembrance.

"While they were eating, Jesus took bread, and when he had given thanks, he broke it and gave it to his disciples, saying, 'Take and eat; this is my body.' Then he took a cup, and when he had given thanks, he gave it to them, saying, 'Drink from it, all of you. This is my blood of the covenant, which is poured out for many for the forgiveness of sins.'" ***Matthew 26:26-28 (CSB)***

A Prayer for Entering

We are thankful, oh Lord, that as we come this day to you and partake of the symbols of your body and your blood, we have personal access to you. We can *enter* into the place of your holiness and receive your body and your blood and be surrounded by your glory. Let us gratefully *enter* and receive all that you have provided for us. In your name we pray. Amen.

As we now take of the bread and the wine, we acknowledge that we are entering into God's presence because the veil of separation was torn and his blood has covered our sins.

Doxology

To you, Oh Lord,
I offer thanks
that through your death,
the veil was torn.
No longer is there separation;
I *enter* your presence with joy.

DAY SEVEN: *COMMUNING WITH CHRIST THROUGH RECEIVING*

As we come to the *Communion Table* as a special time of remembrance, it is important that we think about whom we are remembering and who benefits from *receiving* the emblems of the bread and the cup.

We know it was Jesus who instructed us to remember. He said,

*"This is my body, which is for you; do this in **remembrance** of me…. This cup is the new covenant in my blood; do this, whenever you drink it, in **remembrance** of me." I Corinthians 11:24-25 (NIV).*

Of both the bread and the cup, he told us to **remember** as we eat and as we drink, as we symbolically *receive* into our bodies his body and his blood. So, Christ is glorified in that we take this special time to remember Him.

But what else did he emphasize?

He said, *"This is my body, given for **you**."*

*"This cup is the new covenant in my blood, which is poured out for **you**." Luke 22:19-20 (NIV).*

Think about those words for just a moment and let the truth of them sink in. Jesus said his body and his blood were broken and poured out for **you**!

What wonderful words! What thought-provoking words! What life-changing words! For **you**! Now, let's think of those words in the first person. Jesus' body was broken and his blood was poured out for whom? For **me**! Yes, for **me**! I don't know about you, but when I think about Christ's sacrifice being given so freely for **me,** it touches me deeply; I am overwhelmed! In my spirit, I can hear Jesus say, "**My body was broken for you, my dearly beloved. My blood was poured out for you, my precious one.**"

And those are true statements. His body and blood were offered for **you**! For **me**! However, it doesn't matter what Christ did for us if we don't *receive* his gift. It doesn't mean anything if we don't let his sacrifice become a part of us and change our lives.

We remember that **his** broken body brings healing and wholeness and soundness to **our** bodies; we remember that **his** poured-out blood can figuratively wash over **us**, can bring **us** salvation, and can make **us** new creatures in **him**.

And so today, we worship the one who provided the gift we *receive*. All glory and honor to him who was broken; all praise and adoration to him whose blood was shed!

A Prayer for Receiving

Dear Lord, as we remember we also *receive*. We accept your gift of life – for our bodies, and for our souls. As we *receive* the bread and the cup, we also *receive* your salvation, and your healing, and we praise your name, our Glorious Living Lord. Amen.

And now, as we come to receive the bread and the cup, let us be restored, healed, and made whole as we remember Christ and what he did for us on the cross, giving his life to restore ours.

Doxology

Oh glorious, living Lord,
I accept all that you have for me.
I open my heart, and I stretch forth my hands
to *receive* your peace, provision, and power.
Because you have freely given,
I now come to you
and gratefully *receive*.

DAY EIGHT: *COMMUNING WITH CHRIST THROUGH EXAMINING*

In Paul's words of correction to the Corinthian church regarding *Communion*, one of the things he spoke about was the need for believers to *examine* themselves when coming to the *Lord's Table*. In *I Corinthians 11:28-29 (NIV)*, the passage reads, *"Everyone ought to examine themselves before they eat of the bread and drink from the cup. For those who eat and drink without discerning the body of Christ eat and drink judgment on themselves."* The question then becomes: What does it mean to *examine* ourselves and how do we do it? Many have stated that we must *examine* ourselves to make sure there is no sin in our lives before we come to *The Table*. That sounds reasonable until we consider the fact that not one of us would be invited to partake of the *Lord's Supper* if that were the criteria. Not even the disciples would have been allowed to participate. So again, what is meant by this statement by Paul? He explains by stating that we are to *examine* ourselves to make sure we are properly **discerning** the Lord's body. To **discern** means to understand, to perceive the purpose of, or to take into consideration. So, when we *examine* ourselves to make sure we are correctly **discerning** the Lord's body, we *focus* on Christ's sacrifice, we *reflect* on our Savior's great love for us, and we *exalt* our Lord for his glorious goodness in our lives. This should be our three-fold response as we come to *The Table.*

But when we **are not discerning** the body of Christ, scripture says that we *"...eat and drink judgement on (ourselves)."* The lack of **discerning** becomes a serious defilement of the Lord's Supper. There are several ways we can partake of *Communion* **'without discerning'** so that we meaninglessly or inappropriately participate in *The Supper*.

1) It becomes only a habit; we partake of the emblems as part of an expected routine. (We did it last month, and today is the scheduled Sunday for this month.) We do not conscientiously discern the body and blood of Christ.

2) It becomes a prideful act. We come to *The Table* thinking that we are more deserving to participate than others. We mentally boast of our own righteousness while not considering whether we are in a right relationship with Christ or those in our community of believers.

3) We partake with an irreverent and disrespectful attitude. While the elements are being served, there is whispering, looking around, and cell phone usage taking place. *Communion* is a celebration of God's great love for us, but it also should be a time of reverence and gratitude.

4) We partake of the elements with unbelief. As we eat of the bread and drink of the cup, we do so without acknowledging the truth of salvation and how the cross can bring us victory for today and for all eternity.

The act of *examining* our relationship with Christ and our community helps us to conscientiously and correctly **discern** what he did for us on the cross and gives us a proper prospective from which to enter the place of blessing and partake of the elements as commanded by Jesus himself.

Let us *examine* ourselves as we remember Jesus' words:

"The Lord Jesus, on the night he was betrayed, took bread, and when he had given thanks, he broke it and said, 'This is my body, which is for you; do this in remembrance of me.' In the same way, after supper he took the cup, saying, 'This cup is the new covenant in my blood; do this, whenever you drink it, in remembrance of me.'" **I Corinthians 11:23-25 (NIV)**

A Prayer for Examining

Dear Jesus, you who loved us and gave yourself for us, we come to your table *examining* ourselves that we might properly discern your body and your blood. May we always take of the elements with reverence and gratitude for all that you have done to bring to us salvation. In your name we pray. Amen.

As we carefully examine *our reason for coming to The Table at this Holy Time, let us now take of the bread and the cup together.*

Doxology

As I come reflectively into your presence,
I *examine.*
I *examine* my heart, my thoughts, my motives.
I come to you, discerning your body,
broken and bleeding for me,
and with a humble, grateful heart,
thanksgiving leaps from my lips.

DAY NINE: COMMUNING WITH CHRIST
THROUGH FORGIVING

When we come to the *Communion Table*, one of the things we surely remember is that Jesus Christ our Lord came to die to bring *forgiveness* to our weary, sin-sick souls. His death had a purpose. Out of his fervent passion for his most loved creation, Christ offered *forgiveness* to all who would come to him. In **Ephesians 1:7 (NIV)**, we read, *"In him we have redemption through his blood, the forgiveness of sins, in accordance with the riches of God's grace."* The Greek word for *forgiveness*, *'aphesis'*, means to send away, to release from bondage or imprisonment, to remove as though never committed. Christ gave his blood freely in order to set us free. That freedom comes when we are *forgiven* of our sinful ways, redeemed through Jesus' blood, and liberated in him.

Colossians 1:13-14 (NIV) states, *"For he has rescued us from the dominion of darkness and brought us into the kingdom of the Son he loves, in whom we have redemption, the forgiveness of sins."* The *forgiveness* Christ offers **rescues** us from death; it **redeems** us from destruction; and it **reconciles** us to God the Father. How glorious is his love for us that he would be willing to die that we might be *forgiven*, that he would be obedient in suffering and obedient unto death so that we might be set free!

Daniel 9:9 (NIV) teaches us from the Old Testament that the *"The Lord our God is merciful and forgiving, even though we* *have rebelled against him."* In this Scripture we see that God *forgives* because he is merciful. He *forgives*, not because we deserve *forgiveness*; he *forgives* because of his great love for us. Christ loves us enough to offer *forgiveness*, and the message he sends to us from the cross is one of mercy and grace.

Our responsibility is to receive Christ's redemption which is offered so freely and then in like manner to offer *forgiveness* to those who have trespassed against us. In **Ephesians 4:32 (CSB)**, Paul writes, *"And be kind and compassionate to one another, forgiving one other, just as God also forgave you in Christ."* And in **Matthew 10:8 (NIV)**, Jesus admonishes his followers: *"Freely you have received, freely give."* These words are a good reminder of our need to follow Jesus' teachings, to hear his command, and to obey his instructions in response to the *forgiveness* he has provided to us through his death.

Our *Communion* Scriptures for today come from **Matthew 26:26-28 (CSB):**

"As they were eating, Jesus took bread, blessed and broke it, gave it to the disciples, and said, 'Take and eat it; this is my body.' Then he took a cup, and after giving thanks, he gave it to them and said, 'Drink from it, all of you. For this is my blood of the covenant, which is poured out for many for the forgiveness of sins.'"

A Prayer for Forgiving

Oh, merciful Lord, it is with gratitude that we accept your *forgiveness* and seek to *forgive* others because of the gift you provided for us on the cross. We submit to your cleansing through the cross, to your commandments given for our sanctification, and to your calling that enables us to glorify and proclaim your name. In the Name of the One who loved us and gave himself for us, we offer this prayer. Amen.

Today as we come to the Holy Communion Table, let us be thankful for the forgiveness *of sins, sins washed away by the precious blood of Jesus Christ, the Perfect Lamb of God.*

Doxology

Oh righteous, Holy God,
the one who takes away my sins,
you cleanse me; you set me free
and clothe me with *forgiveness*.
The sin that I once carried
cannot hold me in its sway;
Because I am *forgiven*,
joy dwells in me today.

DAY TEN: *COMMUNING WITH CHRIST THROUGH CLEANSING*

As we come today to partake in the *Lord's Supper*, let us consider the ways sin affected the earth after man's fall in the Garden of Eden and review God's response to that sin. In the time of Noah, sin was rampant. Just like today! God, who is Holy and Pure, could not tolerate what his creation had become so he decided to *cleanse* the earth from sin by sending the flood. His goal was to remove all who were not living in proper fellowship with the Creator as he had planned. He would purge the earth with water, an element that would wash away the horrible, hedonistic sin of the whole world at that time. Except for those who were saved on the ark, all of creation was obliterated but after the flood a promise was made: The earth's inhabitants would never again be destroyed by water to remove the sins of fallen man. Then how, oh how, could the sins of man ever be erased?

God had an answer: He established a covenant with man under which he would require special sacrifices and specific actions that would once again allow man to have fellowship with him, that would again give man access into his presence. And there were rules - many, many rules. But man simply could not keep the statutes that were required under the covenant. Now what? How could man ever again have a relationship with a Holy God? Was that even possible? God said, "Yes, I have a plan. I will make a way." And he sent His Son to be the atonement for the sins of man.

The way the atonement worked was through the death of Jesus, God's one-and-only Son. Jesus' death was harsh. His blood was spilled and flowed from his head, his back, his hands and feet, and from his spear-pierced side. It flowed across the courtyard of the Temple, through the streets of Jerusalem, down the old rugged cross, and spread across the hillside of Golgotha. This blood from God's sinless Son became forever the source of *cleansing* for mankind. *1 Peter 3:18 (AMP)* confirms: *"For indeed Christ died for sins **once for all**, ...so that He might bring us to God, having been put to death in the flesh, but made alive in the Spirit..."* And in *Revelation 1:5 (KJV)*, we read that Christ *"... loved us, and washed (cleansed) us from our sins in his own blood."*

The earth will no longer be *cleansed* by water as in the time of Noah, and God's creation cannot be *purified* through the sacrifice of lambs and goats. No, we **are** *cleansed* by the blood of the perfect Lamb, Christ Jesus, our Lord. His blood is available today to *cleanse* all who put their trust in the one true sacrificial Lamb.

> Yes, the blood of Jesus was spilled for our salvation.
> It was poured out for the washing of our sins.
> It flowed from Jesus' body for our freedom.
> It streamed from his wounds for our *cleansing*.

As the old song proclaims, "Oh, the blood of Jesus; Oh, the blood of Jesus; Oh, the blood of Jesus, it washes white as snow." So, we are washed, we are *cleansed,* because of what Jesus did for us on the cross. And today we want to look back to the work of the cross as we keep Jesus' instruction to remember his death which offers us this beautiful gift of *cleansing*. Let us consider the words of Jesus found in *Matthew 26:26-28 (ESV):*

"Jesus took bread, and after blessing it broke it and gave it to the disciples, and said, 'Take, eat; this is my body.' And he took a cup, and when he had given thanks he gave it to them, saying, 'Drink of it, all of you, for this is my blood of the covenant, which is poured out for many for the forgiveness of sins.'"

A Prayer for Cleansing

Our gracious Lord, we come to you, thanking you for your precious blood that *washes* us, *cleanses* us, and *purifies* us. We are grateful that our crimson sin is changed to blood-washed white when we place our trust in you. We love you and it is in your name we pray. Amen.

As we partake of the emblems, let us once again remember and feel Christ's cleansing power flow through us and over us that we might receive the forgiveness of sin.

Doxology

Oh, Holy One whose blood I see,
May my love forever be,
for you,
the one who *cleanses* me.

DAY ELEVEN: *COMMUNING WITH CHRIST THROUGH RENEWING*

Today our subject is *Communion* as a time of *renewal*. Just think: In the act of coming into Christ's presence while remembering his death on the cross, we can participate in this moment as a time of regeneration of our bodies, our minds, and our spirits. How can this be?

Let's look at the two elements involved in the taking of *Communion* - the bread and the fruit of the vine. What do these signify for our physical bodies? Food and drink, of course - food that gives us nourishment; drink that sustains life. When we eat and drink, our bodies are *renewed*. We gain strength and energy. Our movements are stronger and we feel healthier. Coming to the *Lord's Table* can also bring about the renewing of our bodies. **Isaiah 40:31 (KJV)** tells us that waiting on the Lord *renews* and strengthens us, and as we wait in God's presence during *Communion* and become partakers of the body and the blood of Jesus Christ, he offers healing though his sacrifice on the cross.

Our minds also need *renewal* and in taking time to consider the body and the blood of our Savior, our minds can be restored to *newness* as we kneel in his presence and die to self so that we can put on the mind of Christ. In our *Communion* with Him, we begin to allow our thoughts and desires to be set on him as we share in his sufferings and in his restoration. **Romans 12:2 (RSV)** reads, *"Do not be* *conformed to this world, but be transformed by the renewal of your mind..."* There is not a better time for that to take place than when we come into Christ's presence and remember him by partaking of the elements of *Communion*. We can begin to think his thoughts, act like him, and be filled with his glorious power. *Renewed* minds are better able to proclaim the gospel and live in community with other believers. *Renewed* minds fill us with hope and power!

Spending time in the presence of our Savior also brings about a *renewal* of our inner man. In **Ephesians 4:23 (RSV)**, Paul admonishes that we are to *"... be renewed in the spirit of your minds."*. This relationship we share with Jesus as we partake of the elements of *The Eucharist* has an energizing effect on our spirit by restoring and *renewing* so that as we complete the *Lord's Supper*, we walk away with a clean heart and a sense of being brand new in body, mind, and spirit.

How beautiful is this *Sacrament* of which we are allowed to partake! Out of Christ's death, we have new life. How wonderful to concentrate our thoughts on his words!

"The Lord Jesus on the night he was betrayed took bread, and when he had given thanks, he broke it, and said, 'This is my body which is for you. Do this in remembrance of me.'"

"In the same way also, he took the cup, after supper, saying, 'This cup is the new covenant in my blood. Do this, as often as you drink it, in remembrance of me.'" **I Corinthians 11:23-24 (ESV)**

A Prayer for Renewing

Oh, Giver of Life, we ask for your *renewing* power to rest upon us as we partake of the emblems representing your body and your blood. May our bodies, minds, and spirits be restored as we rest in your presence. As we complete this ceremony of remembrance, let us experience the change that being in your presence brings. In your name we ask these things. Amen.

Now let us be blessed by the renewal you provide as we partake of the bread and the fruit of the vine this day. May our hearts be washed clean, our bodies be healed, and our spirits be renewed as we spend this special time with Christ.

Doxology

Wonderful Savior,
I feel your presence *renewing* me
as I kneel at your nail-pierced feet.
I see the deep and dreadful scars,
and remembering your sacrifice,
I wait before you,
and find I am *renewed*.

DAY TWELVE: *COMMUNING WITH CHRIST*
THROUGH STRENGHTENING

Today as we partake of *The Lord's Supper,* our concentration will center on *Communion* through *Strengthening.*

Andrea Crouch wrote these wonderful, memorable words to the song, *"The Blood Will Never Lose Its Power*":

"The blood that Jesus shed for me
Way back on Calvary
The blood that gives me strength
From day to day
It will never lose its power."

The blood "...gives me **strength**..." are words of truth. In the natural, it is the blood that keeps us alive. It is the blood that touches every organ, every bone, every sinew, and every artery and vein to nourish and to make all body parts viable. **Leviticus 17:11 (KJV)** tells us, *"The life of the flesh is in the blood."*

As believers, our spiritual life is in the blood of Christ. It is his blood that provides us the **strength** to live holy lives, to praise him with our whole beings, and to share his story and his love with others who also need redemption.

The blood of Jesus gives us power. It *strengthens* us to live steadfast, faithful lives; it *strengthens* us to put the works of the enemy under subjection; and it *strengthens* us to rise up in power without fear to declare the truth of the gospel. The power, the *strength,* which Christ exhibited while here on earth, is imparted to us as we partake of his body and his blood. We receive the *strength* to speak, to hear, to see, to act, and to live as Jesus did; his blood brings supernatural power into our lives.

Scripture states in *1 Corinthians 15:2 (NIV)*, *"By this gospel you are saved, if you hold firmly to the **word**." How? "And they overcame him by the blood of the Lamb and by the **word** of their testimony..." **Revelation 12:11 (KJV).*** It is the blood of Christ that gives us the *strength* to speak the Word with overcoming power.

As we accept the power for living that is found in the blood of Jesus and as we symbolically partake of his body and his blood when we come to *His Table*, we can be imparted with his **strength.**   This power can flow through us each day, each moment. We are **strengthened** through the precious blood of Jesus Christ! And we can be **strengthened** by the words he spoke during the first *Communion.*

*"On the night when the Lord Jesus was handed over to be killed, he took bread and gave thanks for it. Then he divided the bread and said, 'This is my body; it is for you. Eat this to remember me.' In the same way, after they ate, Jesus took the cup of wine. He said, 'This cup represents the new agreement from God, which begins with my blood sacrifice. When you drink this, do it to remember me.'" **1 Corinthians 11:23-25 (ERV).***

A Prayer for Strengthening

As we wait in your presence, Lord, help us to realize the power we have because of your blood that was willingly shed. Help us to understand that we can be *strengthened* as we allow ourselves to be cleansed and made strong to accomplish what you have ordained for us to do. In your name we ask. Amen.

Now, let us take the bread and then the cup and feel the Lord's strengthening *power refreshing our bodies and renewing our souls.*

Doxology

Your precious blood I long to feel,
washing over all my sin
to give me life and *strengthen* me;
Your power is offered freely.

DAY THIRTEEN: *COMMUNING WITH CHRIST THROUGH WORSHIPPING*

On this day, I want us to consider *Communion* as *worship*. Often, early in the morning in my quiet time with God, I personally take the elements of the bread and the cup. And as I do, as I remember Christ and what he did for me on the cross, I become overwhelmed with love and gratitude for him because of his great love for me. I reverence, I remember, I reflect, and... I *worship*! I thank God for sending his Son; I thank Christ for His willingness to become my sacrifice; and I thank the Holy Spirit for being present to raise Christ from the dead. As I lift my heart in *worship*, I am drawn into a close, intimate time of *Communion* with the Father, the Son, and the Holy Spirit who all participated in the act of love that bought our redemption.

Today, as we partake of the bread and the cup, I invite you to also use this time of commemoration as a **time of** *worship*. Let us love and adore the One whose body was broken for us. Let us reverence and honor our Lord whose blood was poured forth for us. For he alone is worthy of our honor; he alone is worthy of our praise; he alone is worthy to be glorified; he alone is worthy of our *worship*.

In **Hebrews 12:28 (VOICE),** we read, *"Therefore, let us all be thankful that we are a part of an unshakable Kingdom and offer to God worship that pleases Him and reflects the awe and reverence we have toward Him."*

And in **Romans 12:1 (TPT),** Paul explains what true worship really is. *"Beloved friends, what should be our proper response to God's marvelous mercies? I encourage you to surrender yourselves to God to be his sacred, living sacrifices. And live in holiness, experiencing all that delights his heart. For this becomes your genuine expression of worship."*

So, as we come to the *Lord's Table*, as we solemnly remember his sacrifice, we lift up praises to our Great God. As we *worship* our Savior; let us be showered in thanksgiving for all that He has done.

And as we *worship,* let us hear the words of our Lord when he shared his final *Passover Meal* with his disciples before giving his life to die on the lonely cross.

From **Matthew 26:26-28 (PHILLIPS)**, we can get a picture of the first *Communion*:

"In the middle of the meal Jesus took a loaf and after blessing it he broke it into pieces and gave it to the disciples. 'Take and eat this,' he said, 'it is my body' Then he took a cup and after thanking God, he gave it to them with the words, 'Drink this, all of you, for it is my blood, the blood of the new agreement shed to set many free from their sins.'"

Because we have been set free from our sins, we lift our hearts in *worship*.

A Prayer for Worshipping

Oh Lord our God, as we take of these elements on this new day, we *worship you*. You, who brought us salvation through the shedding of your blood. You, who redeemed us and made us each a new creation. You, our Lord and Savior, Jesus Christ, we *worship You!* Amen.

Let us join together in worship *as we praise him who has loved us from the time of creation. He loved us when he gave up Heaven for us; he loved when he died for us. He loved us when he rose from the dead and ascended back to the Father. He loves us still. Let us now show our love for him. As we partake of the bread and the fruit of the vine, let us* worship.

Doxology

I *worship* from my broken heart;
I worship from my grateful heart
for all that you have done.
You are holy; you are worthy.
I cannot but *worship* you,
Oh glorious, living God

DAY FOURTEEN: *COMMUNING WITH CHRIST THROUGH HEALING*

Today as we come to the *Lord's Supper*, we reflect on *healing* as a part of what Christ provided for us through the horrible injuries, wounds, afflictions and abuses he suffered between the Garden of Gethsemane and the Hill of Golgotha. There, his human voice was temporarily silenced on a cruel cross. The Bible explains in *Isaiah 53:5 (ASV)*: *"But he was wounded for our transgressions, he was bruised for our iniquities; the chastisement of our peace was upon him; and with his stripes we are healed."* **With. His. Stripes. We. Are. Healed!** In *I Peter 2:24*, Peter restates Isaiah's declaration but in the *(NMB),* the verb is translated in the past tense: *"...by his stripes you were healed."* The use of the past tense '*were*' tells us that the work of *healing* had already taken place; it *was* accomplished at Calvary. In the *(TLB)* version, we read, *"For his wounds have healed ours."* Jesus exchanged the wounds he endured (which *were not* deserved) for the many maladies mankind experiences (which *are* deserved). In *Jeremiah 30:17 (NIV)* we are promised, *"'But I will restore you to health and heal your wounds,' declares the LORD."*

At the *Communion Table* we partake of the two elements with which we have become so familiar - the bread (representing the body of Christ) and the wine (representing the blood of Christ). Each one is important and plays a distinct role in the benefits of *Communion* to followers of Christ. We know that Jesus' blood was spilled for our sins, for our transgressions, for our salvation. And we partake of the symbol of Christ's blood in remembrance of his death and the redemption it brings to all who believe.

We partake of the bread as a symbol of Christ's body, broken for us in every conceivable way. He was 'crowned' by sharp thorns; he was flogged, beaten, scourged, scraped and bruised by the roughness of the cross he carried. He was spiked and pierced. Some scholars say Jesus' open wounds were what allowed the sins and the sicknesses of mankind to penetrate the previously sinless and disease-free body of our Savior. He took upon himself the transgressions of all mankind, and he took into his body all the sicknesses, the infirmities, and the disorders that are common to fallen man. Jesus' broken body had a purpose. It was broken for our deliverance from the afflictions of our bodies and minds. It was broken for our *healing*.

Scripture provides examples which help us to comprehend the two-fold blessing, the 'double-cure' we are offered through Christ's death on the cross. *Psalm 103:2-3 (NIV)* reads, *"Praise the Lord, my soul, and forget not all his benefits-who __forgives__ all your sins and __heals__ all your diseases."* And in the *(VOICE, v3)*, *"Despite all your many offenses, he __forgives__ and __releases__ you. More than any doctor, He __heals__ your diseases."* The full verse of *I Peter 2:24 (NIV)* states, *"He himself bore our sins in his body on the cross, so that we might __die to sins__ and live for righteousness; by his wounds you have been __healed__."* And in *Jeremiah 17:14 (NIV),* we read, *"__Heal__ me, Lord, and I will be __healed__; __save__ me and I will be __saved__, for you are the one I praise."*

Through Christ's sacrifice, we can receive both freedom from sin and freedom from sickness.

In remembrance, let us read the *Communion* verses from **Luke 22:19 (TPT):**

"Then he lifted up a loaf, and after praying a prayer of thanksgiving to God, he gave each of his apostles a piece of bread, saying, 'This loaf is my body, which is now being offered to you. Always eat it to remember me'. After supper was over, he lifted the cup again and said, 'This cup is my blood of the new covenant I make with you…'"

A Prayer for Healing

Dear Restoring Lord, we come to *Your Table* today with thanksgiving for your gifts of salvation and *healing*. Thank you for saving us and for the *health* you bring to our bodies and to our minds. In your Holy name we pray, Amen.

Today as we eat of the bread and drink from the cup, let us be especially mindful of the healing that Christ has provided through his death at Calvary. Let us partake together.

Doxology

I receive your *healing* touch.
How could I ask for more
than to be touched by the nail-scarred hand
of the one whom I love and adore?

DAY FIFTEEN: *COMMUNING WITH CHRIST THROUGH PREPARING*

Today we are introduced to *Communion* through *preparing*. In Luke we learn how Jesus himself gave the instructions for the *preparation* of the *Passover Meal* he was longing to share with his disciples. **Luke 22:8-13 (NIV)** reads, *"Jesus sent Peter and John, saying, 'Go and make preparations for us to eat the Passover.' 'Where do you want us to prepare for it?' they asked. He replied, 'As you enter the city, a man carrying a jar of water will meet you. Follow him to the house that he enters, and say to the owner of the house, 'The Teacher asks: Where is the guest room, where I may eat the Passover with my disciples?' He will show you a large room upstairs, all furnished. Make preparations there.' They left and found things just as Jesus had told them. So they prepared the Passover."*

Notice that Jesus had a place in mind for the supper, and he had *prepared* the means for the disciples to find the way. Because of the sorrow that was in front of him, this was to be a special meal. It would be a 'going-away supper' at which the Lord would announce that this would be the last time he would join them at a *Passover Meal* prior to a future 'wedding supper' that he himself would be *preparing* for them. Jesus wanted this to be a remembered meal and he wanted the place and the ceremony to be of great significance to each of them.

Preparation for the Passover Meal was of utmost importance. The location, the proper readying of the food, and the removal of all leaven (sin) from the chosen place were all a part of the *preparation*. The *Passover Meal* was to be eaten at a special time, in a special place cleansed from all leaven, and with the special food required by Jewish law for this annual celebration.

When we partake of the *Lord's Supper*, it is critical that we also make *preparation*. The location and the food (the bread and the wine) are usually *prepared* for us, but it is up to each of us to check the *preparedness* of our own hearts. Are we coming to *The Table* in remembrance, in gratitude, in anticipation, in repentance? We should *prepare* ourselves to take the elements with the right attitude and understanding so that we can properly discern the Lord's body. As we come to the *Lord's Meal* and as we enter his presence by the blood of the Lamb, we are ready to commune.

"He himself bore our sins in his body on the cross, so that we might die to sins and live for righteousness." I Peter 2:24 (NIV). That's why he came; that's why he died. He died that the sin in us might be put to death, and he died that his righteousness might be made alive in us. When we come to the *Lord's Supper*, we are *prepared* (made righteous) because of Christ.

The Lord Jesus gave the instructions for *Communion* as he and his disciples met around the *Passover Table*.

"On the night when Judas betrayed him, the Lord Jesus took bread, and when he had given thanks to God for it, he broke it and gave it to his disciples and said, 'Take this and eat it.

This is my body, which is given for you. Do this to remember me.'

In the same way, he took the cup of wine after supper, saying, 'This cup is the new agreement between God and you that has been established and set in motion by my blood. Do this in remembrance of me whenever you drink it.'" **1 Corinthians 11:24-25 (TLB).**

A Prayer for Preparing

Lord, as we come to receive your gift of grace so graciously given, let us *prepare* our hearts asking for your mercy and seeking your face. In *preparation*, may we understand how blessed we are that your body and your blood offer us forgiveness and healing.

As we prepare to take of these emblems today, let us remember that we are cleansed, we are made righteous because Jesus prepared the way for us to be reconciled to the Father and live eternally with him. Let us be healed from all sin in preparation for the time we spend in the presence of our Savior.

Doxology

As I *prepare* my heart for you,
may any sin that I have carried
be washed away by your precious blood.
May I look to the cross
with thanksgiving and joy
because of the *'place'* you've *prepared.*

DAY SIXTEEN: _COMMUNING WITH CHRIST THROUGH DESIRING_

Communion through _desiring_ is today's topic. Scripture tells us that when Jesus first spoke to his disciples as they gathered around the _Passover Table_, he told them that he had greatly _desired_ to eat this meal with them.

Luke 22:15 (AMPC) states: _"And He said to them, 'I have earnestly and intensely desired to eat this Passover with you before I suffer...'"_ And in **The Passion Translation**, the verse reads, _"Then he told them, 'I have longed with passion and desire to eat this Passover lamb with you before I endure my sufferings.'"_ The words used here by Jesus are strong words: earnestly, intensely, fervently with passion. They give us a sense of just how much he longed to be with those he loved. Before the time of suffering he would endure, he was passionate about being with, and communing with, his disciples.

Why did Jesus make it a point to let his disciples know just how great his _desire_ was to eat this special meal together? I believe in using the word _desired_, he was letting his friends know how great his love was for them. And that great love would soon be exemplified through his suffering, his pain, his great sorrow. _His desire_ was not only to share the meal with them but to complete the task he had been given by his Father so that he could share eternity with them.

Jesus longed to be with his friends and to come together for this special *Supper*. He passionately wanted to spend these last hours with them. Before leaving the room to begin his sorrowful journey to the Garden of Gethsemane, to Pilot's judgement hall, through the streets of Jerusalem, and on to Golgotha, Jesus earnestly *desired* to spend his final hours communing with his friends. He relished the time he could be with them at this moment of communal friendship which would be followed by the greatest act of love anyone would ever bestow. He *desired* to share in *Communion* with his disciples, and Jesus *desires* now to commune with each of us through this special sharing of *His Supper*. What love the Father hath given us that he would lay down his life for his friends!

Is our *desire* to spend time with our Lord remembering his sorrowful sacrifice as great as his *desire* to commune with us? When we come to *The Table*, are we longing to spend this time with the maker of the new covenant? Do we take the time to 'be' with him and earnestly long to feel the warmth of his presence? Jesus *desires* us; let us in return be passionate for him at this Holy time.

"The Lord Jesus, on the night he was betrayed, took the bread, and when he had given thanks, he broke it, and said, 'This is my body, which is for you; do this in remembrance of me.' In the same way, after supper he took the cup, saying, 'This cup is the new covenant in my blood; do this, whenever you drink it, in remembrance of me.'"
I Corinthians 11:23-25 (NIV).

A Prayer for Desiring

Gracious God, we come to you, thanking you that your *desire* to be with us is what brought us back into relationship with you. We now *desire* to spend this time of *Communion* with you, and with grateful hearts we long to be in your presence now and forevermore. In your name we pray. Amen.

By taking the bread and the wine in remembrance of Christ, let us greatly desire *to spend these blessed moments together with him.*

Doxology

Your love poured forth
from your *desire* to 'ever be with me.
I now *desire* to show my love
as I commune with thee.
With the bread and with the cup
I remember you.
Your body crushed,
your blood spilled out,
your covenant to renew.

DAY SEVENTEEN: *COMMUNING WITH CHRIST THROUGH DINING*

On the evening of his arrest, Jesus met with his disciples to share a meal, to *dine* in an upper room which had been prepared for them. Amidst all the inner turmoil and trepidation he was experiencing, and with the somber knowledge of his impending torture and death, Jesus was still thinking of his disciples. He was longing to spend some special time with them, a time they would remember and could relate to long after his death, resurrection, and ascension. What better way to communicate his quickly approaching gift to mankind and his great love for his disciples than through the sharing of a meal!

Coming together to partake of a meal was an important part of the culture of Jesus' day. In this instance, Jesus invited the disciples to join him for a *Passover Meal*. He prepared for it, and then he became the perfect, flawless host, sharing the bread and the wine as a precursor of his journey to the cross where he would willingly offer his body and his blood.to become the perfect, sinless sacrifice. Jesus greatly desired that his disciples would *dine* with him at this time of impending sadness, sorrow, and sacrifice.

For this gathering of Jews, the *Passover Table* was a time of remembrance of the Israelite's release from Egypt's bondage and their freedom from slavery and death. And on this night before Jesus was crucified, the meal became a pattern, a guide for remembering how Jesus came to earth to set us free from the slavery of sin and the darkness of eternal death.

Jesus also invites **us** to *His Table* to share in this special meal. In fact, he doesn't just invite us to *dine*; he bids us come. He summons us to participate in this meal with him. As we eat of the bread (his body) and drink of the cup (his blood), we share an intimate meal with our Savior. We begin to long for more of him, to desire to conform to his image, to share in his death and resurrection enabling us to be dead to sin but alive to Christ.

We are transformed through our *Communion* with Christ, through the act of *dining* at his table.

Dining is a community activity. The *Communion Meal* brings us together with Christ and together with other believers. *The Table* reminds us of Jesus' invitation to *dine*. He calls to us, "Come! Come and *dine* with me." In **John 6:35 (NIV)**, Jesus said, *"I am the bread of life. Whoever comes to me will never go hungry, and whoever believes in me will never be thirsty."*

No hunger! No thirst!

That is Jesus' promise, and each time we **dine** with him we are reminded of that promise. We are spiritually nourished through this *Covenant Meal*, a meal established by Jesus himself and introduced as an ordinance to remind us that we can receive life - life everlasting! How blessed we are to be nourished by Jesus' gifts of his body and his blood!

We read the *Communion* narrative from *I Corinthians 11:23-25 (NIV).*

"The Lord Jesus on the night he was betrayed took the bread, and when he had given thanks, he broke it, and said, 'This is my body which is for you. Do this in remembrance of me.' In the same way also, he took the cup, after supper, saying, 'This cup is the new covenant in my blood. Do this, as often as you drink it, in remembrance of me.' "

A Prayer for Dining

Dear Jesus, Host of *The Meal* we are about to receive, let us *dine* in your presence, realizing that unless you had shared the 'bread of life' and the 'blood of cleansing' with us, we would be dead in trespasses and sin. We praise you for the meal we are about to partake. Amen.

Now, as we share in this meal of the bread and the wine, let us dine with the Giver of Life and be changed as we eat at His Table.

Doxology

As I *dine* on your meal prepared,
my heart explodes with love for you.
Your body, your blood, shared with me,
symbols of your great love for the world.
I am fully nourished as I partake.

DAY EIGHTEEN: _COMMUNING WITH CHRIST THROUGH THANKING_

As we read of the _Last Supper_ as portrayed in Scripture, we see a picture of Jesus and his disciples gathered around the prepared table to participate in the _Passover Meal_. As they were eating, but before he shared with them the bread and the wine, there was one more action he would take: Jesus would first give _thanks_. In _I Corinthians 11:24 (NIV)_, we read, _"... and when He had given thanks, He broke it (the bread) and said, 'This is My body, which is for you; do this in remembrance of Me.'"_

For Jesus, this was a time of _thanksgiving_ for both the Israelite's past deliverance and freedom **and** for the deliverance for all mankind that he would soon provide through his sacrificial death on the cross. Jesus was looking backward with thanksgiving and forward with gratitude. He certainly was not looking forward to the pain and agony that he would soon suffer; he was looking with anticipation and _gratitude_ for the redemption his sacrifice would bring to those he so dearly loved.

When Jesus instituted the _Ordinance of Communion_, he desired that it would be a time of _thanksgiving_. He wanted us to remember him and to be _thankful_ for him and his act of love at Calvary.

One of the words we use for *Communion* is *Eucharist*. It is the English version of the Greek word, '*eucharisteo*', which means to be grateful, to feel *thankful*. When we share in the *Communion Meal*, we show our *thankfulness* for the body of Christ that was broken for us and his blood that was poured out for us as symbolized by the bread and the wine. Because of what *Communion* celebrates, it is intended to be a *thanksgiving* supper.

When we partake of the elements, we are reminded to be *thankful* for our salvation, to be *grateful* for the life we have in Christ, to *rejoice* in the liberty we find through him, and to *delight* in the joy we can experience because of the great gift Jesus so freely gave. Paul calls this gift of redemption an *"indescribable gift."* In **The Voice** version of **II Corinthians 9:15**, the verse is translated, *"Praise God for this incredible, unbelievable, indescribable gift!"*

How can we not be *thankful* for a gift so wonderful it cannot even be described?

When we come to the *Eucharist Table*, we are by our actions saying '*thank you*' for all that Christ has done. Our being there, our act of showing up at the table, our participation in the remembrance of his crucifixion and death, together turn this moment into a *thanksgiving* feast.

This *thanksgiving* feast invites us to think of the many things Christ did for us for which we can be *grateful*, and as we do, our spirits become one with our Savior's. A holy presence joins us together in uniting with Christ and in uniting us with each other, and we worship you with *gratitude*.

Scripture reads in *I Corinthians 11:24-26 (NIV),*

"... and when he had given thanks, he broke (the bread) and said, 'This is my body, which is for you; do this in remembrance of me.' In the same way, after supper he took the cup, saying, 'This cup is the new covenant in my blood; do this, whenever you drink it, in remembrance of me. For whenever you eat this bread and drink this cup, you proclaim the Lord's death until he comes.'

A Prayer for Thanking

We are *thankful* for you, our Lord and Savior, and for the life we can experience because of all you did for us on the cross. How marvelous is your wonderful, indescribable gift! Help us to be forever *grateful* for your eternal, everlasting love. Amen.

And now, as we partake of the symbols of Christ's gift to us, may this act become a thanksgiving praise to our glorious Lord.

Doxology

Oh, giver of body and blood,
my love for you grows larger
as I offer *grateful* praise.
And in your presence,
I experience *eucharisteo.*

DAY NINETEEN: <u>*COMMUNING WITH CHRIST THROUGH BREAKING*</u>

In today's devotional, our discussion centers on *breaking*. When Jesus sat down with his disciples on the eve of his crucifixion, they first shared in the *Passover Meal.* Scripture tells us in **Matthew 26:26 (NIV)** that, *"While they were eating, Jesus took bread, and when he had given thanks, he broke it and gave it to his disciples, saying, 'Take and eat; this is my body.'"*

At this time in history, the *breaking* of a loaf of bread into smaller pieces was the usual way for it to be shared. The Greek word for *breaking*, '*klao'*, is better understood as *tearing apart* the bread, and that is how Jesus passed the bread around - he tore it into smaller pieces and then he shared it. Not everyone would be able to partake of the bread unless it was *broken.* Leaving the bread in one full loaf would not feed each of the disciples of its goodness. It had to be *broken* in order for it to be shared.

Jesus said that the bread was his body; He equated the *breaking* of the bread to his soon-to-be *broken* body. And just as he blessed the bread, he also blessed his body. *"...Jesus took the bread and when he had given thanks (blessed it), he broke it..."* In **John 17:1,3 (NLT),** Jesus gave thanks for his own body that would soon be *broken.* He blessed the **restoration** that eating natural bread brings, and he blessed the **redemption** that partaking of his torn body brings to those who receive. He said, *"Father, the hour (for the breaking of my body) has come. Glorify your Son so your Son can give glory back to you.... And this is the way to have eternal life—to know you, the only true God, and Jesus Christ, the one you sent to earth."*

Here Jesus was saying, "**Break** me, crucify me, so that through the *breaking* of my body, salvation will come to God's creation and the Father will be glorified." Just as the bread is *broken* and given for the sustaining of man's life here on earth, Christ's body was *broken* and given that man might have eternal life with Him. His body, like the bread, had to be *broken* so that it could be shared that many might come to him and live - really live!

Isaiah 53: 4-5 (KJV) gives us a picture of how Jesus' body was *broken* for us. *"Surely he has borne our griefs and carried our sorrows; yet we did esteem him stricken, smitten of God, and afflicted. But he was wounded for our transgressions, he was bruised for our iniquities;..."*

He was smitten, afflicted, wounded, bruised. He was *broken* so that our **brokenness** could be mended, that our sin-injuries could be healed. He endured the horrible, crushing *breaking* so that we might be made whole.

Broken bread. *Broken* body. Each blessed; each shared.

And now as we read the *Communion* Scriptures from **I Corinthians 11:23-25 (NIV),** let us remember Christ's broken body and his poured-out blood.

"The Lord Jesus, on the night he was betrayed, took the bread, and when he had given thanks, he broke it, and said, 'This is my body, which is for you; do this in remembrance of me.' In the same way, after supper he took the cup, saying, 'This cup is the new covenant in my blood; do this, whenever you drink it, in remembrance of me.'"

A Prayer for Breaking

Dear Lord, as we come to this time of *Communion*, let us remember that you were willing to be *broken* for us, that your body received the wounds that bring healing to our bodies, minds, and spirits. Let us receive your gift of *brokenness* that we might be made whole. Amen.

We now partake with grateful hearts of the symbols of Christ's body that was broken and his blood that was spilled for our redemption.

Doxology

Your Holy body, *broken* for me
gives hope for all eternity.
It was the *breaking* and the blessing
that makes me whole,
that sets me free.

DAY TWENTY: *COMMUNING WITH CHRIST THROUGH COMMITTING*

Communion through *committing* is our subject for today. In our society, when we speak of *commitment*, the word marriage usually comes to mind because that is one of the greatest *commitments* we as human beings ever make. But today we will be discussing another term that is similar to marriage - betrothal. Betrothal is not a commonly used word in our modern day, western culture, but in Jesus' day it was a well-known tradition which defined a solid, pre-wedding *commitment* between a man and a woman. Though much like our custom of announcing an engagement before a wedding is planned, the betrothal was much more significant. It was considered to be an unbreakable agreement; it was a *commitment* which was to be taken seriously by both parties and was to be a covenant agreement, a binding contract between the man and the woman. Bible scholars say that the betrothal was comparable to marriage but the couple would not live together or consummate the marriage until the wedding took place at a later date. That is how serious the betrothal *commitment* was.

When a young man proposed to his beloved by pouring out and offering a cup of wine to her, he was asking for her hand in marriage. If she drank from the cup offered, she was agreeing to become his bride. But it was a choice; she could drink of the wine or push the cup away and leave the ceremony without entering into the covenant relationship with her pursuer.

When Jesus sat down with his disciples for a *Passover Meal* on the night he was betrayed, he made a **commitment** to them. When he said, *"This cup is the new covenant in my blood"* **Luke 22:20 (NIV),** and offered it to them, he was letting his disciples know that he was making a promise; he was *committing* to them, making a covenant with them, for a future 'wedding'. He was inviting them into an intimate union so that they could be with him forever.

With these words and the sharing of the wine, Jesus was making a non-revocable offer to his future bride.

And the disciples responded to this 'proposal' by drinking from the cup. They said, "Yes." They knew they wanted to be with Jesus forever, to live with him and to be with him as part of his Kingdom so it was easy to agree to this covenant Jesus was offering them. Even though they didn't fully understand, they knew they wanted to accept Christ's invitation.

Each time we come to the *Communion Table*, each time we participate in the symbol of betrothal, we are **recommitting** to being forever with Christ. We are saying, "Lord, I accept your life and I offer mine in return. You are mine and I am yours. I want to be in covenant fellowship with you until we are together, face-to-face. I want to be your bride."

Remember the words of Jesus.

"'This is my body, which is given for you. Do this in remembrance of me.' In the same way, he took the cup of wine after supper, saying, 'This cup is the new covenant between God and his people—an agreement confirmed with my blood. Do this in remembrance of me as often as you drink it.'" **I Corinthians 11:24-25 (NIV).**

A Prayer for Committing

Lord Jesus, today we *commit* to you - all that we are, all that we have, all that we can be as we renew our covenant with you. We love you, Jesus, with all our hearts, and it is in your name we pray. Amen.

As we eat of the bread and drink from the cup, let us pledge, let us commit ourselves, to our future Bridegroom.

Doxology

You are my love and I am yours;
how I long to be with you.
I see your arms are open wide
calling me to your house.
I do not know when you will come;
I do not know the day or the hour.
But this I promise, my betrothed,
I *commit* to watch for you.

DAY TWENTY-ONE: _COMMUNING WITH CHRIST THROUGH LIVING_

When we come with discernment to the _Lord's Table_, we understand our need for him. We confess our dependence on him. We look to the cross and realize that without Christ there is no salvation, there is no growth in holiness. Indeed, without Christ there is no _life_ at all, either physically or spiritually.

Acts 17:28 (NIV) states quite succinctly the truth regarding our physical _lives_. _"For in him we live and move and have our being."_ **_Galatians 2:20_** teaches us that because we are _"crucified with Christ"_ we also have him _living_ in us. In the **_(VOICE)_** translation, it becomes clearer: _"I have been crucified with the Anointed One— I am no longer alive—but the Anointed is living in me; and whatever life I have left in this failing body I live by the faithfulness of God's Son, the One who loves me and gave His body on the cross for me"._ Yes, we are his creation and have _life_ in our bodies of flesh because of him.

Regarding our spiritual lives, Jesus has quite a bit to say. He states that in order to be spiritually alive with him we must believe in him as Savior and follow him as Lord.

And we must figuratively be willing to take into our bodies his body and his blood. In *John 6:53-58 (TPT)*, we read his own words: *"Listen to this eternal truth: Unless you eat the body of the Son of Man and drink his blood, you will not have eternal life. Eternal life comes to the one who eats my body and drinks my blood, and I will raise him up in the last day. For my body is real food for your spirit and my blood is real drink. The one who eats my body and drinks my blood lives in me and I live in him. The Father of life sent me, and he is my life. In the same way, the one who feeds upon me, I will become his life...Eat this Bread and you will live forever!"* It is the sacrifice of the body and the blood of Christ which brings us into eternal *life*.

Communion reminds us of our need for both elements. Without the nourishment of food and drink, life ebbs away in the physical as well as in the spiritual realm. We need to partake of both to stay physically whole, and we need to partake of the bread and the cup of *Communion* in order to stay healthy in our spiritual nature. When we fail to eat symbolically of the body of Christ by placing our trust in him, belief can be weakened in our hearts and in our souls so that no spiritual *life* can be found in us. When we decline to accept by faith the bountiful benefits provided to us through the blood of Jesus, we turn down the glorious offer that brings us eternal *life*. As we read *I Corinthians 15:54, 57 (NLT),* we begin to understand the truth of the eternal *life* found in Christ.

"...when our dying bodies have been transformed into bodies that will never die...he gives us victory over sin and death through our Lord Jesus Christ." What a blessed gift of *life* we receive because of Calvary!

And now we contemplate the words of Jesus spoken in the Upper Room when he established the *Ordinance of Communion.* *"The Lord Jesus, on the night he was betrayed, took bread, and when he had given thanks, he broke it and said, 'This is my body, which is for you; do this in remembrance of me.' In the same way, after supper he took the cup, saying, 'This cup is the new covenant in my blood; do this, whenever you drink it, in remembrance of me.'"* **I Corinthians 11:24-26 (NIV).**

A Prayer for Living

Gracious Lord, we accept the *life* you offer through your death on Calvary's cross. We come to you with grateful hearts, understanding that it is through your death that we can have eternal *life*. We thank you that when the time comes and we are in your eternal presence, there will be no more separation, no more sadness, no more sickness, no more scarcity. There *will be life* everlasting and fullness of joy forevermore. We are grateful for your gifts and honor your great name. Amen.

Let us partake of the bread and drink of the cup as we remember Christ's wonderful gift of life.

Doxology

Dear Jesus Christ, you offer *life*
through your death on a cruel cross.
I now give my *life* to you.
I praise and bless and honor you.
Because of your unfailing love,
I can truly *live*!

DAY TWENTY-TWO: *COMMUNING WITH CHRIST THROUGH SHARING*

As we come to the *Lord's Table* and read from *I Corinthians 10:16-17 (NLT),* we are reminded that when partaking of the cup and the bread during *Communion*, we are in actuality participating in a time of *sharing.* *"When we bless the cup at the Lord's Table, aren't we sharing in the blood of Christ? And when we break the bread, aren't we sharing in the body of Christ? And though we are many, we all eat from one loaf of bread, showing <u>that we are one body</u>."*

Not only are we *sharing* in the blood and body of Christ **with him,** but we are also *sharing* in the body and blood of Christ **with fellow believers.** It is the *sharing* that makes *Communion* such a time of intimacy. Partaking of the elements as instructed by our Lord draws us into Christ's presence together to share in the act of love that brought redemption to our souls. By *sharing* in the blood and body of Christ and by partaking of *His Special Meal*, as believers we also *share* together in the promises echoed in Scripture.

We *share* in his sufferings; we *share* in his death. We are called to do this. Because we join with Christ in his suffering and death, we are also invited to *share* in the many benefits that he has promised. We *share* in his blessings, we *share* in his comfort, and we will *share* in his resurrection. We will *share* in his Kingdom (we will reign with him); we will *share* in his glory. And we will *share* eternal life with Christ, our Lord.

86

Let's look at some of the New Testament Scriptures to help us gain a better understanding of the promises we as a community of saints can *share* with each other as we *share* with Christ.

In *Ephesians 3:6 (ERV),* **w**e find that all true followers of Christ *"...are part of the same body, and they share in the promise God made through Christ Jesus."*

Paul states in **Romans 6:5 (VOICE),** *"...if we (believers) have been united with Him (Christ) to share in a death like His, don't you understand that we will also share in His resurrection?"*

And in **Galatians 2:20 (AMP),** we read, *"...I have been crucified with Christ (that is, in Him I have shared His crucifixion); it is no longer I who live, but Christ lives in me.*

In *II Timothy 2:11-12 (TPT),* we see that the *sharing* (joining together) in Christ's death (defeat) brings us together with him in his triumph. *"If we were joined with him in his death, then we are joined with him in his life! If we are joined with him in his sufferings, then we will reign together with him in his triumph."*

"We share in the terrible sufferings of Christ, but also in the wonderful comfort he gives". II Corinthians 1:5. (CEV)

"He (God) is the one who chose you to share in his own kingdom and glory." I Thessalonians 2:12. (CEV) states, *"We will also share in the glory of Christ, because we have suffered with him." Romans 8:17. (CEV)*

It is amazing that because we *share* in Christ's <u>sufferings</u> and <u>death</u>, we can also *share* in his <u>*glory*</u> and enjoy <u>eternal life</u> with him.

As we come now to *The Table* to *share* in the bread and the wine symbolizing the body and blood of our Lord, let us be reminded that in return Christ *shares* all good things with us. As we *share* with our Lord the horrors that were in inflicted on him through his <u>*death*</u> on the cross, he will someday bring us to his side to *share* in the magnificence of his <u>*resurrection*</u> and <u>*glory*</u>.

And now we read the words of Jesus spoken on the night before his crucifixion. *"This is my body given for you; do this in remembrance of me." This cup is the new covenant in my blood, which is poured out for you."* **Luke 22:19,20 (NIV).**

A Prayer for Sharing

Oh Lord, you have allowed us to *share* in your death that we might also *share* in your glorious life and in your Kingdom. Today we worship you. Help us to remember that your blessings are unlimited and eternal. In your name we pray. Amen.

Let us now partake of the bread and the wine as a symbol of sharing in Christ's sufferings and death.

Doxology

I am grateful for the *sharing*
of your body and your blood.
For in the *sharing,*
I receive
life everlasting.

DAY TWENTY-THREE: *COMMUNING WITH CHRIST THROUGH FELLOWSHIPPING*

As we come together to partake of the *Lord's Supper* in accordance with the instructions given by our Lord on the night he was betrayed, let us reflect on *Communion* as an act of *fellowshipping.*

Luke 22:14 (TLB) speaks of the meal shared by Jesus and his disciples. *"Then Jesus and the others arrived, and at the proper time all sat down together at the table..."* Notice: *"They **all** sat down **together!"*** They came together for a *Supper* that would be a time of *fellowship.*

There are several things to consider about this evening:

1) Jesus did not partake of the emblems by himself. He had his group of disciples with him to join in this Holy time of *Passover.* It was a time of *fellowship.*

2) The occasion was special in that it celebrated a historical event, the time Israel as a national **community** was freed from the tyranny of the Egyptians.

3) It was a time of remembrance and reflection on the goodness of God to His people.

4) It was a time of *Communion*, commitment, and caring
    – *fellowship*!

5) It was a solemn yet joyful occasion.

6) It brought the group **together** at a special time for a
    special reason.

7) It was a scene that continues to be replicated by
    those who love and serve our Lord. All these many
    years later, we come, and we *fellowship*.

The word *Communion* really means *fellowship*.
Fellowshipping is what Jesus and his disciples were doing that
special night before Christ went to the Garden of Gethsemane
and then on to the cross. And that is what we do when we
come together to observe the *Lord's Supper*. We meet in the
same room or through the same venue; we reflect on the
same story – the story of Christ's death and what it means to
us; we partake of the same emblems, those that remind us of
Christ's body and his blood; and we do this together, in
fellowship, in *Communion*.

What an important time! We join in this special moment to
remember all that Christ did for us on the cross. I can almost
see the Son of God smiling as we **join** as a community of
believers to remember him. The cross brought us back into
Communion with God, and the celebration of what Jesus did
for us on the cross continues to bring us into *fellowship* with
our Creator and with each other.

Philippians 3:10 (KJV) speaks of this *fellowship*: *"That I may
know him, and the power of his resurrection, and the
fellowship of his sufferings,..."* As we participate in Christ's

sufferings through *Communion*, we can know him more intimately and experience treasured *fellowship* with him. We are a blessed people. How wonderful it is to *fellowship* with each other as we remember our Lord's sacrifice that brought us back into *fellowship* with the Father!

Let us remember Christ's words recorded in *I Corinthians 11:24-25 (VOICE)* *"This is My body, broken for you. This cup is the new covenant, executed in My blood."*

A Prayer for Fellowshipping

Dear Lord of *Passover*, we are so grateful that we can meet in your presence as a community of believers to *fellowship* together and to *fellowship* with you as we take these emblems. We worship you, Jesus our Savior, who brought us back into *fellowship* with our Holy God, our Creator. We thank you, in Jesus' name. Amen.

Let us now fellowship with our Christ and with fellow believers as we partake of the emblems and remember him.

Doxology

Oh, Lord of Communion,
How very blessed I am
to be a part of your great *fellowship*.
Your love envelopes us -
together.
I gladly commune with you.

DAY TWENTY-FOUR: _COMMUNING WITH_
CHRIST THROUGH UNITING

Communion through _uniting_ is our subject for today. Regarding the taking of _Lord's Supper_, the Apostle Paul had some choice words to say when he learned that many followers of Christ were using the celebration of _The Supper_ in an 'unworthy manner'. The unworthy manner about which Paul spoke was the actions by some of the Corinthian Jews who were setting up 'classes' among themselves based on their financial, cultural, political, and religious statuses. This affected the ability of some who desired to participate and was causing great division among those who were coming together to partake of the _Passover Meal._ Because the bread and wine were taken along with a full meal, some of the members would arrive early, drink heavily, and gorge themselves having no consideration of those in the lower levels of society who would come later to find nothing was left for them to eat including the elements needed for _Communion._ The elites were not using this time to remember Christ's suffering and death. No! They were having a party!

And so, Paul called them out on this. He said in _**I Corinthians 11:20, 22 (VOICE)**_, _"...when you come together...it is not the Lord's Supper you are eating at all... Do you have so little respect for God's people and this community that you shame the poor at the Lord's Table?"_ Lack of reverence for Christ and lack of respect for many of his followers caused division

93

instead of the *unity* and harmony which Jesus had in mind when he shared the elements with his disciples. Paul would have none of it!

As Christians today, we should be compelled to listen to Paul's words and realize how incongruous were the actions of the Corinthians with the *unity* the Lord's Supper was meant to signify. Jesus himself had fashioned it as an institution of fellowship when he met with the disciples in the Upper Room. As he prepared and shared the meal, he made it obvious that people of all backgrounds could come into his presence and commune with him. Think of the people who met with Jesus that night. There was a tax collector, a few fishermen, a zealot (politician), probably some tradesmen who had become his followers, and a deceitful money manager. Many of them would have fallen into the category of the 'poor' Paul spoke about. And yet they had been with the One who was the originator of the *Ordinance of Communion*. Jesus wanted them to **come together** in *unity*. He wanted them to prepare **together**, to meet **together**, to eat **togethe**r, to pray **together**, to partake of the bread and the cup **together**, and to sing **together** before heading out to the Mount of Olives. This was to be a time of **togetherness**, a time of *unity*.

In *I Corinthians 10:17 (VOICE)*, we get the full picture: *"Because there is one bread, we, though many, are also one body since we all share one bread."* We are to come together in *unity* as we share Christ, the Living Bread. We are to be open and caring for all believers, treating each with respect and love. When we do this, we are showing love and reverence and obedience to Jesus Christ our Lord, the giver of his body and his life's blood.

And now, we read from *I Corinthians 11:23-25 (VOICE).*

"On *the same night the Lord Jesus was betrayed, He took the bread in His hands; and after giving thanks to God, He broke it and said, 'This is my body, broken for you. Keep doing this so that you and all who come after will have a vivid reminder of me.' After they had finished dinner, He took the cup and in the same way said, 'This cup is the new covenant, executed in My blood. Keep doing this; and whenever you drink it, you and all who come after will have a vivid reminder of me.'"*

A Prayer for Uniting

Lord, we come to you in the spirit of *unity* that we may be one in you. Let us today acknowledge your power to bring us *together* under your Lordship that we may function as that one body to which you have called us. We pray these things in your name. Amen.

As we now take of the bread and the cup, let us be *united* under the banner of the love of Jesus Christ, the Bread of Life.

Doxology

Unity with others, Lord,
as I commune with you.
May your love pour over us,
sacredly *uniting* us,
as your emblems we partake
at this Holy time.

DAY TWENTY-FIVE: *COMMUNING WITH CHRIST THROUGH BEHOLDING*

Today we study *Communion* through *beholding*. In the Gospel of John, in the very first chapter, John exclaims to those around him, *"Behold the Lamb..."* John knew Jesus was coming and he was prepared to see him, to *behold* him, and to introduce him as the Lamb of God to those who were now his own followers. And so, when Jesus approached, John cried out:

"This is the one I was talking about when I said, 'Someone is coming after me who is far greater than I am, for he existed long before me.'" John 1:15 (NLT). And in *John 1:29 (ESV)*, John shouted, *"Behold the Lamb of God, who takes away the sin of the world."* John had received a vision of who Jesus was. He had *beheld* the glory of the Lamb when he baptized Jesus in the Jordon River, and he understood the preeminence of this God-man who had entered their world. Now the time had come for John to announce Jesus' identity to those around him. *"The following day John was again standing with two of his disciples. As Jesus walked by, John looked at him and declared, 'Look, the Lamb of God!' When John's two disciples heard this, they followed Jesus." John 1:35-37 (NLT).*

Do you see what *beholding* Jesus does? It directly affects all that we do. When John's followers realized who Jesus was, when they *beheld* him, they left John and followed Jesus.

Paul in *II Corinthians 3:18 (ESV)* states, *"Beholding the glory of the Lord, (we) are being transformed into the same image..."* *Beholding* Christ brings change; it transforms every part of our being, enlivening us to become more like him.

When we take *Communion*, it is important that we consider Jesus on the cross, that we *behold* him there and contemplate all that he did for us. See him hanging there, suffering shame. *Behold* his nail-scarred hands, his feet. See the blood pour from his side. *Behold* the Lamb, sacrificed for you, for me. *Behold* the Lamb, *"...slain from the foundation of the world."* **BEHOLD THE LAMB OF GOD!**

As we spend time *beholding* Jesus and as we follow his instructions given on the night he shared the *Passover Meal* with his disciples, we can be changed, transformed, made holy in his presence. We remember him and *behold* him as the *"...author and finisher of our faith"* through his gift provided for us at Calvary. Let it be so!

And now we read the words spoken by Jesus as he instituted the *Ordinance of Communion*:

"The Lord Jesus, on the night he was betrayed, took the bread, and when he had given thanks, he broke it, and said, 'This is my body, which is for you; do this in remembrance of me.' In the same way, after supper he took the cup, saying, 'This cup is the new covenant in my blood; do this, whenever you drink it, in remembrance of me.'" **I Corinthians 11:23-25 (NIV).**

A Prayer for Beholding

Holy God, we look to you and see your glory because you have opened our eyes to truly *behold* who you are. We *behold* you on the cross, and someday we will *behold* you face to face. We will *behold* you in all your glorious splendor as you reign as King of Kings and Lord of Lords. We are so grateful that you want us to see you and to know you. In your name we pray. Amen.

As we now take of the emblems, as we eat of the bread and drink from the cup, let us behold *Christ as Savior and* behold *him as Lord.*

Doxology

I *behold* you, Lamb of God.
I see you on cross.
Remembering your great love for me,
I am transformed by you
and long to see your face.

DAY TWENTY-SIX: *COMMUNING WITH CHRIST THROUGH IDENTIFYING*

Today, as we come to the *Lord's Table*, I want us to reflect on the *Lord's Supper* as a time of *identifying*. In **Galatians 2:19-20 (NCV)** Paul explains: *"It was the law that put me to death, and I died to the law so that I can now live for God. I was put to death on the cross with Christ, and I do not live anymore—it is Christ who lives in me. I still live in my body, but I live by faith in the Son of God who loved me and gave himself for me."*

In these two verses we are introduced to the concept of being crucified with Christ. Paul says, *"I was put to death on the cross **with Christ.**"* Not physically on a cross; we did not literally hang there and suffer and bleed with him. But symbolically, it was as though we had been nailed to the cross with our Lord so that our sin might be blotted out. **Our. Sin. Gone. As though we had never committed it.**

By accepting Jesus' death as the provision for our sin, we can *identify* with Christ as our old nature, our sinful nature, dies. Man was strangled by the law and condemned by the law which brought with it a penalty that needed to be paid. When Jesus was crucified, our debt, our penalty, was paid just as though we had been put to death for our own sin. But we didn't have to die; Jesus died in our place. And now the law no longer has power over us to condemn us. The law could not save us, and now it cannot pass judgement on us. We have the ability to die **to** our sins because Jesus died **for** our sins. We *identify* with his death on the cross as though we had been on Golgotha's Hill dying with him.

Can you imagine being put to death in such a cruel manner? As you visualize the scene at Calvary, can you see the cross with Jesus hanging there, nearly lifeless, smitten and broken? Can you hear the taunts of the enraged soldiers who despised him and the mournful cries of those who loved him? Can you *identify*? Can you imagine having your head 'crowned' with sharp thorns, your shoulders and back scourged and bleeding, your side pierced, your hands and feet spiked to the cross? Your heart broken? Can you *identify*?

On this day as we come to the *Communion Table,* let us meditate on what Christ did for us on the cross. Let us remember that he took our place so that we might die to sin and no longer be condemned to death. Let us *identify* with the One who became our substitute so that we might be raised to new life in him. In *I Peter 2:24 (DLNT),* we read, *"Who Himself bore our sins in His body on the cross in order that we, having died to sins, might live for righteousness."* When Jesus hung on the cross, it was our sins that put him there, and it was our sins that kept him there. Oh, what love! Oh, what a Savior!

Today we *identify* through participation: *I Corinthians 10:16 (ESV)* reads, *"The cup of blessing that we bless, is it not a participation in the blood of Christ? The bread that we break, is it not a participation in the body of Christ?"* As we partake of the cup and the bread, we *identify* with the blood and the body of Christ.

As we come to *The Table*, let Jesus' words touch our souls.

"'This is my body, which is for you; do this in remembrance of me...This cup is the new covenant in my blood; do this, whenever you drink it, in remembrance of me.'"
I Corinthians 11:24-25 (NIV).

A Prayer for Identifying

Oh God, we are here in your presence to remember you and *identify* with what you experienced on Calvary's cross. Because of your great love for us, our sins are washed away, and we can be made dead to sin and all the ravages and heartache and sorrow it brings. Now, wonderful Lord, we can be alive to your power and to your glory. We thank you and we praise your name. Amen.

As we now take of the bread and the cup, we identify with our great substitute, Jesus, our Lord and Savior.

Doxology

Dear Lord, I see you on the cross.
Your blood flows down;
I cannot watch.
As I *identify*, I see
that I'm the one 'should be there.
But because of your great love
I walk in freedom, sins erased.
Your dying has brought me life.

DAY TWENTY-SEVEN: *COMMUNING WITH CHRIST THROUGH RECOGNIZING*

Today we recall the story recorded in **Luke 24:18-31** of two travelers on the road to Emmaus who failed to *recognize* Jesus after his death and resurrection. They were walking along and talking about the week's events and all that had taken place before their very eyes. Suddenly they were accompanied by a third person, someone they did not *recognize*. Scripture reveals it was Jesus, the one who was the front-and-center character of these strange *Passover* happenings. But the travelers did not know him; they did not *recognize* him. When Jesus asked what they were discussing, they thought it strange that anyone who had been in Jerusalem at this time would not be aware of the many unusual events carried out by the governing and religious leaders of the day.

Even when Jesus talked about the Old Testament Scriptures relating to these events, the travelers did not know who he was but as they came near the village, they invited him in to dine with them. It was while they were at the table and Jesus began to break the bread that they finally *recognized* him as their friend. They *recognized* him because they had seen him break bread before. By his physical appearance, they had not recognized him. By his words, they had not understood who this co-traveler was. But by the action of him breaking the bread, they suddenly came to understand that this co-traveler was Jesus: *"Then their eyes were opened, and they recognized him."* **v.31 (CJB)**

When we take *Communion*, it gives us the opportunity to fully *recognize* Jesus as the Christ, our Great Sin-Bearer. We remember and consider that he broke the bread as a symbol of his broken body, and he invites us to eat of the bread and to partake of his body in *recognition* of who he is in the plan of redemption.

Every time we come into the presence of Jesus and participate in *Communion*, we should find ourselves in a deeper relationship with him. We *recognize* him as the breaker of bread, the giver of his body, broken for us. We recognize him as our life-sustainer through his blood that was spilled for our redemption. Being in his presence during this Holy time reminds us that he broke the bread to symbolize his own broken body, and we *recognize* him. We really see him! He offers life to us, his blood-bought children. He is all we need.

Let us remember his words on the night he was betrayed.

"He took some bread in his hands. Then after he had given thanks, he broke it and said, 'This is my body, which is given for you. Eat this and remember me.'"

After the meal, Jesus took a cup of wine in his hands and said, This is my blood, and with it God makes his new agreement with you. Drink this and remember me.'" **I Corinthians 11:23-25 (CEV).**

A Prayer for Recognizing

Lord Jesus, as we take of the emblems you have established for us, help us to *recognize* you for who you are and remember we can continually live in your presence because of the sacrifice you made at Calvary. As we eat of the bread, let us contemplate your body, your Holy, human body that was broken for us. Let us partake and let us remember. Thank you for your sacrifice, oh Lord Most High. In your holy name we pray. Amen.

As we take of the emblems, let us recognize our Savior and remember all that he has done for us.

Doxology

You, my Christ, show me your love.
As bread is broken in your hands,
your broken body bids me see
that you are present;
you are *recognizable!*

DAY TWENTY-EIGHT: *COMMUNING WITH CHRIST THROUGH ACKNOWLEDGING*

Each time we come to the *Lord's Table* and partake of the Communion elements, it becomes an *acknowledgement* of our relationship with Christ. When we correctly, with discernment, participate in the fellowship of his suffering and contemplate his death on the cross, we say that we believe all that the Bible declares. First of all, we *acknowledge* that Christ is God, the Second Person of the Trinity. We affirm by our presence at the *Communion Table* that we believe Jesus died on a cross to save us from sin and to someday take us to live with him eternally in Heaven. We say that we are his followers and want to come in obedience to him to remember him in *The Eucharist*. There we are reminded that Christ's death is the only death that will ever be needed to bring us back to God. We *acknowledge* that salvation by any other means or through any other man is not necessary **nor** is it possible. Christ paid our debt once and for all, and through his blood that was spilled on the cross, every sin committed can be washed away. As we come to the *Lord's Supper*, we specifically *acknowledge* three things:

We *Acknowledge* and *Commemorate* the *Past*.

> We believe all that Scripture tells us about Jesus is true. He came as a baby, was conceived by the Holy Spirit, born of a virgin, walked among men. He taught in the temple, healed the sick and distressed, raised the dead, and

controlled the natural elements. He caused a great uproar among the ruling classes so much that they decided to put him to death. He suffered horribly before dying on a cross, shamed, bleeding and broken for our sins. Jesus' Father turned his back on him, and he was buried in another man's grave. But the Holy Spirit was present to raise Christ from the dead, and he ascended into Heaven to be with the Father in his proper place of prominence. That is the *past* we **commemorate**.

We *Acknowledge* and *Celebrate* the Present.

We believe that in our lives today, Jesus is present through the Holy Spirit. When we remember Christ's death, we *acknowledge* that we, according to scriptures, can share in his **crucifixion**, his **burial**, his **resurrection**, and his **life**. We see proof of this in verses from the **Christian Standard Bible (CSB):** *"I have been **crucified** with Christ, and I no longer live..."* **Galatians 2:20;** *"Therefore we were **buried** with him by baptism into death, ". **Romans 6:4);*** *"He also **raised us up** with him and seated us with him in the heavens." **(Ephesians 2:6);*** *"The **life** I now **live** in the body I **live** by faith in the Son of God, who loved me and gave himself for me." **(Galatians 2:20);*** *"Now if we **died** with Christ, we believe that we will also **live** with him." **(Romans 6:8);*** and, *"... just as Christ was **raised** from the dead by the glory of the Father, so we too may walk in newness of **life." (Romans 6:4).*** In the ***present***, we **celebrate** Christ's presence in our lives.

We *Acknowledge* **and** *Confidently Anticipate* **the Promise.**

We believe in the words Jesus spoke about our future lives with him. He said he would return for us and bring us into his Kingdom and that he would not share the bread and the cup again until that special time. In ***John 14:2-3 (ASV)***, we read, *"I go to prepare a place for you. And if I go and prepare a place for you, I will come again, and receive you unto myself; that where I am, there you may be also."* ***Philippians 3:20 (PHILLIPS)*** tells us that *"...we are citizens of Heaven; our outlook goes beyond this world to the hopeful expectation of the Savior who will come..."* And in ***II Timothy 4:18 (NIV)***, we are promised that *"The Lord...will bring me safely to his heavenly kingdom."* What a wonderful expectation for a glorious future with our radiant King!

As we *acknowledge* the Christ who was, and is, and is to come, let us read the words he spoke on the night he was betrayed.

"As they were eating, Jesus took bread, blessed and broke it, gave it to the disciples, and said, 'Take and eat it; this is my body.' Then he took a cup, and after giving thanks, he gave it to them and said, 'Drink from it, all of you. For this is my blood of the covenant, which is poured out for many for the forgiveness of sins.'" ***Matthew 26:26-28 (CSB)***

A Prayer for Acknowledging

Great and Mighty Savior, we *acknowledge* you. We *acknowledge* who you are, what you did, that we can have fellowship with you, and that our future is fulfilled in you because of your death at Calvary. Thank you for dying for us. In your name we pray. Amen.

Let us now partake of the bread and the cup as we acknowledge Christ.

Doxology

I *acknowledge* you, my Lord,
and what you did for me
to make me whole, to set me free,
through your death at Calvary.

DAY TWENTY-NINE: _COMMUNING WITH_
CHRIST THROUGH FINISHING

In the Upper Room, Jesus shared the _Passover Meal_ with his disciples and introduced them to the _Communion Sacraments_. His words of admonition, teaching, instituting, and warning followed by a prayer were to become known as the Upper Room Discourse. Scripture tells us that, _"When Jesus finished praying, he went with his followers across the Kidron Valley. On the other side there was a garden (Gethsemane), and Jesus and his followers went into it." **John 18:1 (NCV).**_ Jesus had _finished_ his instructions and was now heading to a place where he would again pray, this time not for his disciples but for himself only. He would seek the Father's guidance in the decision he would have to make as he contemplated the horrible sorrow and pain he would soon endure. It was a stressful, heart-wrenching prayer. In **_Luke 22:45 (TPT),_** we read that,_" He prayed even more passionately, like one being sacrificed, until he was in such intense agony of spirit that his sweat became drops of blood, dripping onto the ground."_ And then, _"When he finished praying, he went to his followers... (and)... found them asleep..." **Luke 22:45 (ERV).**_ Feeling all alone, the burden grew heavier still.

But it was on the cross right before he died that Jesus' final words were spoken when he declared, "It is _finished._" Jesus had accomplished his planned actions, _finishing_ them one step at a time. In each of these instances, Jesus raised his voice to his Father, crying out for help. Help my disciples; help me; help many to benefit through my *finished* work.

There is a common theme in each of these –the blood of Jesus. While reclining around the table in the upper room, Jesus spoke of the **wine being his blood**. He said, *"This cup is the new covenant between God and his people—an agreement confirmed with my blood, which is poured out as a sacrifice for you." **Luke 22:20 (NLT).*** In the garden, his **sweat became drops of blood.** And as Jesus was hanging, dying, **offering his life's blood** on the cross, we read, *"After Jesus had taken the wine (sour vinegar), he said, 'It is finished.' Then he bowed his head and released his spirit." **John 19:30 (ESV)***

The Greek word for *finished* is **tetelestai,** which can also mean 'it has been accomplished', 'it is completed', 'it is fulfilled', or 'paid in full'. Jesus certainly fulfilled all that he had come to do, and he paid in full the sin-debt that should have been ours. Because, *'it is finished'*, there are no longer blood sacrifices required, we are free from guilt, we have no more shame, and we have the promise of eternal life with God.

We are forgiven; we are free; we are forever favored by God.

IT. IS. FINISHED!

Communion is a declaration of the *finished* work of Christ. The Upper Room is the place Jesus began his trip to the cross and it is there that he taught us to continually remember him through the *Ordinance of Communion*.

In *I Corinthians 11:24-26 (NIV)*, Paul shares with us Jesus' words spoken on the night before his crucifixion:

"The Lord Jesus, on the night he was betrayed, took bread, and when he had given thanks, he broke it and said, 'This is my body, which is for you; do this in remembrance of me.' In the same way, after supper he took the cup, saying, 'This cup is the new covenant in my blood; do this, whenever you drink it, in remembrance of me.'"

A Prayer for Finishing

Savior of the world, we come to you with grateful hearts because you were willing to *finish* on the cross what was necessary to blot out our sins and bring us to eternal life with you. We are so grateful that you didn't leave the upper room deciding not to die. We are thankful that you obeyed the Father's will in the Garden of Gethsemane, and we come amazed into your presence for the *finished* work of Calvary that you willingly accomplished on our behalf. Amen.

As we today eat of the bread and drink of the cup, let us be gloriously aware that our sins are gone because Jesus completed the assignment given to him by his Father. Let us remember that he finished the commission to bring love and grace to his fallen creation.

Doxology

You paid my debt in full;
you washed away my sins.
You *completed* what you came to do
when you cried out from the cross,
"It is finished."
I thank you and adore your Name.

DAY THIRTY: _COMMUNING WITH CHRIST THROUGH GLORIFYING_

As we today come to the _Lord's Table_, our discussion centers on _Communion_ as _glorifying_. In **John 17:1-5 (ESV)**, we read part of a farewell prayer offered by Jesus. This appeal was expressed not only for the benefit of his disciples but for his own benefit as well. Christ used wording which pointed directly to what he would soon accomplish on the cross. Jesus had been teaching his followers about the trouble that would certainly come to them, and understanding his own 'trouble' was close at hand, he lifted his eyes to Heaven and prayed, _"Father the hour has come; **glorify** your Son that the Son may **glorify** you, since you have given him authority over all flesh, to give eternal life to all whom you have given him. And this is eternal life, that they know you, the only true God, and Jesus Christ whom you have sent. I **glorified** you on earth, having accomplished the work that you gave me to do. And now, Father, **glorify** me in your own presence with the **glory** that I had with you before the world existed."_

To _glorify_ means to clothe in radiance, to reveal one's splendor, to expose the significance of. And in these verses recorded by John, we see Jesus praying that through the Father, this _glorification_ would be given to him, the Son. The purpose? That the _glory_ expressed in Christ would also _glorify_ the Father. And then Jesus said that through his *glorification* those entrusted to him would receive eternal life and forever be with him.

The Bible clearly teaches that eternal life is only possible through Jesus' death on the cross so now we begin to understand that the *glorification* of the Son was brought about not by Jesus being lifted up and crowned as a radiant king but by his being raised up on a cruel cross to be mocked and die as a common criminal. *His glorification was received through his crucifixion.* Why would Jesus pray to be crucified? Why would he pray to receive the pain of a rugged cross over the pleasure of Heaven and the glory surrounding his Father?

It turns out that the way back to his Father and the *glory* of Heaven was through the cross. So, when Jesus was praying to be *glorified*, he was praying to go home; he was praying to be reunited with his Father and be covered with the same **glory** that had been his before the world existed. And through his *glorification*, Jesus accomplished what no other man could accomplish: He made it possible for the Father to be *glorified* through him, for his creation to know him intimately and to *glorify* him, and for all those given to him to have eternal life and be in his *glorious* presence forever.

As we come to the time of *Communion* today, and as we survey and remember the cross, we offer *glory* to the Son whose life and death brought *glory* to the Father. And we *glorify* the Son by remembering. We lift him up as one of significance, one covered in radiance, one filled with splendor. He is the *glorious* shining gift to all mankind.

We read in *I Peter 2:22, 24 (VOICE), "The Anointed One suffered for us and left us His example so that we could follow in His steps. He took on our sins in His body when He died on the cross so that we, being dead to sin, can live for righteousness."*

And we are reminded that at the *Communion Table* that Jesus, *"... took bread, gave thanks and broke it, and gave it to them, saying, 'This is my body given for you; do this in remembrance of me.' In the same way, after the supper he took the cup, saying, 'This cup is the new covenant in my blood, which is poured out for you.'" Luke 22:19-20 (NIV).*

A Prayer for Glorifying

Oh, King of our Hearts, you are significant and worthy. Your spender outshines all others, and we now come to *glorify* you as we partake of your body and your blood. Thank you for your great love for us. It is in your name we pray. Amen.

As we partake of the elements today, let us be thankful and joyful for what Christ accomplished for us on the cross. Let us glorify *him.*

Doxology

Be *glorified*, oh Christ, my Lord,
as I partake of your body and blood.
Let me never forget how much you gave
and all that was accomplished
through your wondrous love.
I lift you up; I raise you high.
I'm in awe of your *glorious* radiance.

DAY THIRTY-ONE: *COMMUNING WITH CHRIST THROUGH ANTICIPATING*

When we come to the *Lord's Table* to partake of *Communion*, we look **backwards** to the cross, **remembering**. And in the **present**, we share in *Communion* by **participating** in the meal of the bread and the wine. But we are also to look **forward**, *anticipating* a future *Communion* called The *Marriage Supper of the Lamb.* Jesus spoke of this coming event when he first instituted the *Ordinance of Communion*. In **Luke 22:15-18 (ESV)**, we read his words, *"And he said to them, 'I have earnestly desired to eat this Passover with you before I suffer. For I tell you I will not eat until it is fulfilled in the kingdom of God.' And he took a cup, and when he had given thanks he said, 'Take this, and divide it among yourselves. For I tell you that from now on I will not drink of the fruit of the vine until the kingdom of God comes.'"*

It's clear that the disciples really did not understand the meaning of the future kingdom about which Jesus spoke. They didn't realize that this statement also foretold that he would soon die, be resurrected and then return to the Father. But Jesus wanted to share these words with them anyway so that in the future they would remember them and begin to understand about the glorious Kingdom plans God has for those who accept his great gift of love and follow him.

Part of the story of the Kingdom is the *Wedding Supper of the Lamb* as described in **Revelation 19:7,9 (ESV)**. *"'Let us rejoice* *and exult and give him the glory, for the marriage of the Lamb has come, and his Bride has made herself ready.' And the angel said to me, 'Write this: Blessed are those who are invited to the Marriage Supper of the Lamb.'"* Those who are invited to this special supper are called **'blessed'**, as it will be a feast like no other. Jesus introduced us to a forerunner of this great feast when he established the *Ordinance of Communion*. The *Lord's Supper* is a rehearsal, a wedding rehearsal, for our soon-coming marriage and we are to rehearse this future wedding until our Bridegroom comes.

The one who was the *"**Lamb** slain from the foundation of the world"* …, *"the **Lamb** of God, who takes away the sin of the world…,"* becomes the Bridegroom at the *"Wedding Supper of the **Lamb**."* The Lamb, the one who loves us like no other, who died for us and freed us from our sins, will one day bring us to himself in the most intimate relationship that could ever be imagined. Yes, the Lamb becomes the Bridegroom, the Husband of the Church, his Bride.

We who are in right relationship with Christ are the Bride and should be *anticipating* our coming marriage. Remember, when we partake of the *Lord's Supper*, we are rehearsing and looking forward to spending eternity with our beloved, our glorious Bridegroom. Participating in *The Eucharist Meal* encourages us to keep our eyes on our Bridegroom and to keep our 'wedding garments' pure and white so that when we meet at the feast we will be properly adorned for our husband. Our *anticipation* should grow with every *Communion Meal* in which we participate.

We remember the words of Jesus on the night he was betrayed: From **Mark 14:22-24 (NCV)** we read:

"While they were eating, Jesus took some bread and thanked God for it and broke it. Then he gave it to his followers and said, 'Take it; this is my body.' Then Jesus took a cup and thanked God for it and gave it to the followers, and they all drank from the cup. Then Jesus said, 'This is my blood which is the new agreement that God makes with his people. This blood is poured out for many.'"

A Prayer for Anticipating

Lord Jesus, as we partake of the symbols of your body and your blood, we look forward with *anticipation* to that glorious day when we shall enjoy the greatest meal of all, the *supper* provided for us by you, our Lamb and our Bridegroom. We love you and thank you for loving us. In your Holy name we pray, Amen.

Let us now partake of the bread and the wine that symbolize Christ's body and Christ's blood. And as we partake, we rehearse and anticipate our future wedding meal with Christ, our beautiful, beloved Bridegroom. Let us glorify Him!

Doxology

As here before your throne I kneel,
I accept the bread and drink the wine.
With open eyes and open heart,
I *anticipate* the marriage feast.
I am yours and you are mine.

AFTER THE CROSS

In my mind's eye,
I see the cross;
I see the Lamb of God once slain.
The blood that flowed from flesh so torn
now makes me whole, rids every stain.

I hear the taunts;
I hear the pounding
of the spikes through hands and feet
that held my Savior to the cross,
or so they thought.

Yes, He did die; the spear made sure.
His side was pierced, and life drained out.
It was all over; death had won,
or so said some.

But then comes Sunday,
that third day!
The grave is empty;
What now say they?

The angels said,
"He is not here."
The light shown bright
and caused great fear.

But Mary stayed
and heard the voice
of Him who caused her to rejoice.
She ran to tell those who had left,
"He is not dead; our Master lives!"

How wonderful to hear such news!
And still this truth rings through the years.
Our God's not dead; He lives today
and longs for us with Him to stay.

He's coming back to take His bride,
and forever we'll abide
with the One who gave His life,
and then...,
arose triumphant over sin!

Soon I shall hear the trumpet sound!
No force on earth can hold me down.
I'll rise to meet the Great I AM.
Glory to the Risen Lamb!

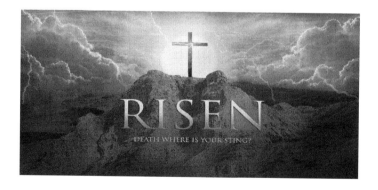

Made in the USA
Lexington, KY
13 December 2019